Eat to beat cholesterol

Nicole Senior APD & Veronica Cuskelly

NEW HOLLAND

First published in Australia in 2007 by
New Holland Publishers (Australia) Pty Ltd
Sydney • Auckland • London • Cape Town

1/66 Gibbes Street Chatswood NSW 2067 Australia
218 Lake Road Northcote Auckland New Zealand
86 Edgware Road London W2 2EA United Kingdom
80 McKenzie Street Cape Town 8001 South Africa

10 9 8 7 6 5 4 3

National Library of Australia Cataloguing-in-Publication Data:

Senior, Nicole
       Eat to beat cholesterol: how to lower your cholesterol and enjoy delicious food.

       Bibliography
       Includes index.
       ISBN 9781741104493

       1. Low-cholesterol diet - Recipes. 2. Food - Cholesterol content.
       I. Cuskelly, Veronica. II. Title.

       641.56311

Publisher: Fiona Schultz
Managing Editor: Martin Ford
Editor: Jenny Scepanovic
Project Editor: Lliane Clarke
Designer: Gregory A Lamont
Photography: All recipe photographs Vicky Liley. Meat & Livestock Australia (page 101),
Dairy Australia (page 115), Australian Mushroom Growers' Association (page 49), Accent Creations (page 106)
Production: Monique Layt
Printer: SNP/Leefung Printing Co Ltd (China)

Nutritional analysis used SERVE Nutrition Management System Version 5.2.001 based on AUSNUT database.

Although every effort has been made to ensure that the contents of this book are accurate, it must
not be treated as a substitute for qualified medical advice. Always consult a qualified medical practitioner.
Neither the authors not the publisher can be held responsible for any loss or claim arising out of the
use, or misuse, of the suggestions, or the failure to take medical care.

Front cover from left to right: Chargrilled Salmon (p220), Apple with Scrunched Filo (p240), Sardine on Rye (p196)
Back cover form left to right: Watermelon in Rosewater (p234), Salmon, Tandoori Chicken (p216)

Having a healthy heart
means you can grab hold of life
with both hands.

—Nicole and Veronica

Acknowledgements

Books just don't happen. This book would not have been possible without help from many people who were generous both with their time and their expertise. In particular, we would like to thank the following dietitians for their feedback and input: Andrea Mortenson from Meat and Livestock Australia, Barbara Eden from the National Heart Foundation, nutrition consultant Bill Shrapnel, exercise physiologist Caitlin Reid, Claire Palermo from St Vincents Hospital Sydney, Dr Susanna Holt, Jacinta Orr from Dairy Australia, Lisa Yates from Nuts for Health, and Meaghan Ramsey and Megan Cobcroft from Unilever Australasia.

We are very grateful to Professor Jennie Brand-Miller from the University of Sydney, Professor Sandra Capra from the University of Newcastle and to Trish Griffiths from Go Grains, BRI, for their invaluable assistance.

Thanks also to Ian Hemphill of Herbie's Spices for sharing his spice blend secrets in our chapter on Herbs and Spices.

We are grateful to our publisher Fiona Schultz for giving us the opportunity to write this book and for her faith in us, Lliane Clarke and Jenny Scepanovic, our editors, for bringing this book to life, and Vicki Liley for her beautiful food photography.

And without our colleague Philippa Sandall we wouldn't have written this book together at all. Thank you for your encouragement and editorial expertise from day one.

From Nicole: Thank you to the wonderfully talented Veronica Cuskelly, whose magic has made all the nutrition theory come alive to tempt the senses in her fabulous recipes. Your enthusiasm, positivity and expertise are so appreciated.

A thousand thanks go to my husband Liam for his support and understanding during all the lost weekends buried in research and writing. Also to my family and friends for their unending faith, and to all my clients, family and friends whose high cholesterol inspired me to take action.

From Veronica: Nicole's quirky, energetic writing style made me realise from the outset that this was going to be a nutrition book with a difference. Her dedication and commitment to good nutrition being all about deliciously tasting food and expert nutritional guidelines for recipes made the journey of this book evolving a great joy.

A huge thank you to my partner, Andrew, for tasting and critiquing the recipes during development and to my family and friends for always hastily accepting invitations to enjoy my culinary creations.

Contents

Part 3:
Eat to beat
cholesterol in your kitchen 137

Appendices

Introduction

Heart-friendly food is good for the whole family

Food really is the best medicine, yet we live in a world where healthy food is not always the easiest choice, and the cost of drugs to lower cholesterol and reduce heart disease risk are spiralling out of control. The evidence is good for the protection afforded by heart-friendly foods and eating patterns. Physical activity and a healthy diet are as potent as any drug to promote heart health, and form part of a total package of wellness that has many other benefits for the individual and the nation.

We wrote this book to tip the balance towards healthy food, and hopefully in a small way make a difference to the alarming and devastating statistics of heart disease. Food is nature's gift for us all to enjoy, and good food can help us be happy and well. We hope this sensible, practical and accurate information about enjoyable eating for a healthy heart will help make healthy living a reality for you and yours.

How to use this book

In Part 1: You and your heart, we set out the facts about heart disease and why it's so important to make change for the better. We explain why lowering cholesterol, managing your weight and being physically active are so important.

In Part 2: Say hello to heart-friendly foods, you will discover the truly delicious world of heart-friendly foods—what you need to know about them and how much you need to eat. And to make it easy we have included lots of 'Quickies'—fast and easy ideas for including these super heart foods in your daily diet.

Part 3: Eat to beat cholesterol in your kitchen, is the practical part, with eating plans, cooking tips, shopping lists and delicious recipes for breakfast and brunch, light meals, main meals, desserts and snacks—all with nutritional information per serve.

Most of all we hope you enjoy the journey of learning about the healing and protective powers of food, as well as the fun and satisfaction of preparing heart-healthy meals, snacks and desserts.

—Nicole Senior & Veronica Cuskelly

Part 1

You and your heart

1: Why focus on cholesterol?

By lowering your blood cholesterol, especially the bad LDL type, you can make a real difference to your long-term health and wellbeing.

High blood cholesterol increases your chances of having a heart attack. Cardiovascular disease (heart attack and stroke) is the biggest killer of Australians and New Zealanders. The higher your cholesterol, the greater your cardiovascular risk.

The heart is the body's engine room, nourishing every organ, muscle, nerve and bone with oxygen and nutrient-rich blood. So, look after your heart and you can spend more time doing the things you enjoy, be able to fully participate in life with no restrictions, be around to enjoy your children and grandchildren, and live to see more great places and people. We have written this book to help you beat cholesterol by eating better and moving more.

Facing the facts

1. In Australia, the proportion of people with high cholesterol has not improved in the last 25 years. And if you're thinking high cholesterol only affects other people, think again. At last count, one in two adult Australians and 60 per cent of adult New Zealanders had above ideal cholesterol levels.

2. Age is no barrier.
It's not just oldies. We now see signs of heart disease (fatty streaks in the arteries) in older children and teenagers—especially if they are overweight. Because children learn what and how to eat from their parents, heart-healthy eating starts with those first foods.

3. The lower your cholesterol level, the lower your risk of heart disease.

How do we know this? One of the most well known, long-term scientific studies of heart disease and lifestyle is the Framingham Heart Study, based in Massachusetts USA. It started in 1948 when researchers recruited 5000 people and followed them and their families over three generations assessing their health, eating habits and activity levels every two years. From all the data collected we now know that the major risk factors for cardiovascular disease are:

- high blood cholesterol, high triglycerides and low levels of the good HDL cholesterol
- high blood pressure
- smoking
- obesity
- diabetes
- physical inactivity

as well as risk factors like your age and gender and having a family history of heart disease. And while you can't change your age or family history, you can take control of your cholesterol, especially the bad LDL type (see page 17).

4. Lowering your cholesterol naturally with food rather than drugs means you will save on the nation's enormous drug bill!

Cholesterol-lowering drugs are a substantial part of Australia's government subsidised drugs scheme, the Pharmaceutical Benefits Scheme (PBS). In 2001, lipid lowering drugs were the most heavily prescribed drug group in the PBS. They now cost close to a billion dollars a year and still growing.

Framingham risk tables predict that lowering LDL cholesterol by 20% reduces cardio-vascular risk by about 25% over five years.

How low do you go?

So you've had your cholesterol tested and your doctor says it's fine; do you still need this book? Yes. The lower your cholesterol level, the lower your risk of heart disease—even if your cholesterol level is within the 'acceptable range'. So what next? Research has shown that eating a diet rich in heart-friendly foods and moving a bit more can lower cholesterol without the side effects of drugs.

Heart-friendly foods are a powerful ally in the fight against cholesterol

Your supermarket and fresh produce market shelves are piled high with heart-friendly foods so you won't find eating this way adds to your shopping bills. Fresh vegetables, fruits, fish, nuts, seeds, lean meats and low fat dairy foods all the way through to wholegrain breads with added folate, low fat milk with added calcium and omega-3, and healthy oil-based spreads enriched with plant sterols. And don't forget tea, red wine and dark chocolate!

2: The heart of the matter

Cardiovascular disease is still the biggest killer of both men and women. In short, the way we live is causing a large number of us to become sick, disabled or die before our time.

There is a lot we can do

So what's the solution? Is there anything we can do? The answer is a resounding yes! The majority of heart disease is preventable. The solution lies in the food on our plates, and the miles on our dials. High blood cholesterol and the risk of heart disease can be reduced by enjoying a healthy combination of heart-friendly foods and getting moving.

Prevention is better

For those who have already had a heart attack, it is possible to substantially reduce the risk of having another one by making lifestyle changes; but, of course, preventing heart attacks in the first place is the best result of all.

Having a family history of heart disease increases your risk of developing it; however, although you can't change your family or your genes, you can change your lifestyle. You can significantly reduce your risk by taking control of the way you eat and the way you live. Healthy living doesn't mean boring food and punishing gym workouts! It's about enjoying more heart-friendly foods like vegetables, wholegrains, fruits, fish, nuts and healthy oils and being more active on a daily basis, such as walking more.

What is heart disease?

Cardiovascular disease (CVD) is the collective term for hardened arteries and blocked blood vessels that cause heart attacks and strokes. Heart attacks are a large part of the CVD problem and are the end result of blockages in the arteries nourishing the heart—called coronary heart disease (CHD). These vital blood vessels become narrowed and then eventually blocked in a process called atherosclerosis (hardening of the arteries).

How to look after your heart

The best chance of keeping you heart healthy is to work on reducing or removing the risk factors you can change. Taking control of your lifestyle can increase the length and quality of your life. And in a lucky coincidence, changing your lifestyle for the better also improves your general wellbeing and reduces your risk of other serious diseases.

1. Talk to your doctor about a CVD risk assessment.
2. If you smoke, get help to quit.
3. Keep tabs on your cholesterol levels over time.
4. Control your blood pressure.
5. Enjoy a healthy diet low in saturated fat and salt with plenty of heart-friendly foods.
6. Put together at least 30 minutes of moderate physical activity every day.
7. Maintain a healthy weight and waist (lose weight sensibly if you need to).
8. If you have diabetes, maintain good blood glucose control.
9. If you drink alcohol, do so in moderation.
10. Actively manage stress.

What is atherosclerosis?

Atherosclerosis is a complex process. Put simply, the hardening of blood vessels occurs because of a build-up of fat, cholesterol and other substances inside blood vessels. It is the bad LDL form of cholesterol that is most to blame. What makes things worse is LDL cholesterol undergoes oxidation—a process similar to metal rusting if left out in the weather. This build-up of oxidised LDL then causes inflammation as the body tries to defend itself; similar to the redness and swelling when you get a splinter in your finger. The end result is a hardened and inflamed 'plaque', which can make the artery narrow and block it completely—especially if a blood clot gets stuck—causing a heart attack (myocardial infarction, or MI).

What are the main risk factors for heart disease?

There is no one cause of heart disease, rather factors that if present together increase the chance of athero-sclerosis and heart attack. Below are the risk factors—the more you have, the higher your risk. Some you can't change, but there are many you can.

Preventable risk factors	Unavoidable risk factors
Tobacco smoking	Being older
High blood pressure	Being of Aboriginal or
High blood cholesterol	Torres Strait Islander
Insufficient physical activity	descent
Overweight and obesity	Being of Maori or Pacific
Poor nutrition	Islander descent
Heavy alcohol use	Being male
Diabetes and pre-diabetes	Being from the Indian
Stress	subcontinent

- Around half of Australian and New Zealander adults have high cholesterol levels
- More than half Australians and New Zealanders are overweight or obese (more men than women)
- One in five Australians and New Zealanders are obese
- Around half Australians and New Zealanders are insufficiently active for health (less than 30 minutes a day, five days a week)

Women and heart disease: the menopause connection

Heart disease is still the biggest killer of women in Australia. Heart disease kills four times more women than breast cancer. While women share the same risky levels of blood cholesterol, blood pressure, overweight and physical activity, female hormones offer some protection up until menopause. After menopause, however, all the trouble starts, and heart disease really takes hold. Research from the USA shows women don't do as well after a heart attack and are more likely to have a second heart attack, become disabled or die early than men. While women often have the role of caring for others in the family, it is vital they take control of their own health for a long and healthy life.

Assessing your risk

After the age of 45 years (men) and 55 years (women), you must have your level of CVD risk assessed by your doctor. If you have diabetes, you already know you have risk factors, or if you're from a higher risk ethnic group, you need to start 10 years younger.

High risk—what now?

The aim is to reduce your absolute risk. Your doctor will recommend you improve your lifestyle no matter what your risk level, and this means enjoying a heart-friendly diet, regular physical activity and managing stress. Your doctor will recommend other forms of therapy such as medication and more regular follow-ups, the higher your risk. For some people, diet may not be enough.

Being treated with medication to lower your CVD risk is no reason to give up on heart-healthy eating. Diet and medication work together to provide additional benefits.

What is the metabolic syndrome?

The metabolic syndrome (also known as syndrome X) is the description given to the unlucky coincidence of having several risk factors for disease at the same time. Having metabolic syndrome dramatically increases the risk of CVD, as well as the risk of developing type 2 diabetes.

A key feature of the metabolic syndrome is having insulin (a hormone) that doesn't work effectively, a condition called insulin resistance.

You have the metabolic syndrome if you have:

* Too much fat around your middle
  Waist circumference (European, East Mediterranean, Sub-Saharan African): 94 cm or more for men or 80 cm or more for women.
  Waist circumference (South Asian, Ethnic Central and South American): 90 cm or more for men and 80 cm or more for women.

Plus any two of the following:

* High triglycerides more than 1.7 mmol/ or treatment for this.
* Low HDL (good) cholesterol less than 1.03 mmol for men and less than 1.29 mmol/L in women, or treatment for this.
* High blood pressure: Systolic BP 130 or more and Diastolic BP 85 or more, or treatment of previously diagnosed high blood pressure.
* Raised fasting blood glucose level more than 5.6 mmol/L, or previously diagnosed type 2 diabetes

If you have the metabolic syndrome, you need to focus on reducing the impact by losing weight, lowering your triglyceride levels and blood pressure, and increasing your HDL levels. A heart-friendly diet and being more active will help enormously.

What is insulin resistance?

Insulin resistance is the condition where insulin does not work effectively. Insulin normally helps the body to use the glucose circulating in your bloodstream after you have eaten for energy by helping it to enter cells. In a state of insulin resistance, less glucose can get into cells and more stays in the blood. The body works harder to compensate by producing more insulin, but to no avail. Having high insulin levels significantly increases the risk of heart disease, and encourages weight gain.

High blood glucose levels increases CVD risk

In another example of the too-close-for-comfort association between blood glucose level and heart disease, researchers from the US followed over 1000 adults over 8–10 years and found those with higher long-term blood glucose levels (measured as HbA1c)—even without diabetes—had almost double the risk of heart disease. The risk of having thickened (hardened) arteries measured by ultrasound was two and a half times higher in those with the highest HbA1c than those with the lowest. The association between HbA1c and CVD risk has also been found in similar studies in Europe.

Strategies for lowering blood glucose levels, such as physical activity, losing weight and enjoying a low GI diet also reduces the risk of heart disease

Stress is bad for your heart

Although instinctively we have known that stress is bad, scientific evidence has emerged quite recently supporting stress as a significant risk factor for heart disease. Chronic anxiety, depression and anger are widely recognised as raising the risk of heart attack. 'Stress' is a broad term, but we all instinctively know what it means. Constant work stress, social isolation, anxiety, depression and upsetting events all contribute to an increased risk of heart disease. Being a type A personality is also a risk, typified by anxiety and hostility.

Becoming aware of the signs of stress and actively managing personal triggers is an important component of good health

The physiological response to stress was originally quite helpful. The so called fight or flight response—an adrenalin rush, faster heartbeat and the release of stored fuel into the bloodstream—allowed us to survive threats by fighting back or running away quickly. The problem is, nowadays the threats are more mental than physical but our body still reacts the same. Put simply, our body is ready to run but has nowhere to go, and so instead turns in on itself and causes damage.

Stress can directly impact on the heart by increasing blood pressure and the chance of blood clots, but it can also influences our behaviour. During stressful times we tend to focus on the short term and live 'hand-to-mouth' rather than think about what we're doing. For many people this means making less healthy food choices, overeating and not making time for exercise.

Stress-busters

- Eat a variety of nutritious foods regularly through the day.
- Take time out for movement or exercise.
- Avoid too much caffeine and alcohol.
- Maintain a good sleep routine.
- Talk to others—share your thoughts and worries.
- Schedule some 'down time' to do nothing much but reflect and daydream.
- Take up yoga, or practise meditation.
- Breathe deeply and slowly into the belly.
- Build some fun into your day.
- Practise self-nurturing activities: such as massage or a bath.
- Practise saying 'no' to unreasonable demands.
- Practise positive thinking.

3: The cholesterol connection

While you can't change your age or your family history, you can take control of your cholesterol—especially the bad LDL type.

What is cholesterol?

Cholesterol is a fatty, waxy substance essential to life. It's found naturally inside our bodies, and has a number of useful purposes. It is used as a structural component in cell membranes, as a raw material to make sex hormones, vitamin D, and bile that helps digest fats. Most cholesterol is made in the liver, but we can also obtain cholesterol from food. Cholesterol and other fats in the blood are collectively known as blood lipids, and when they are high the medical term is hyperlipidaemia.

Why the bad reputation?

Cholesterol becomes a problem when there's too much of it. High levels of blood cholesterol are a risk factor for heart disease, but it also spells trouble for blood vessels elsewhere in the body such as in the brain leading to stroke, and in the legs leading to peripheral vascular disease. High cholesterol levels are also linked with diabetes and high blood pressure. Some types of cholesterol are worse than others.

The different types of cholesterol

Cholesterol is transported around the body attached to proteins and cholesterol particles called lipoproteins. Different lipoproteins have different effects on heart disease risk.

The main type to worry about is Low Density Lipoprotein, or LDL cholesterol. This is the bad type of cholesterol whose main job is to take cholesterol from the liver to be deposited in blood vessels, become oxidised, and then cause atherosclerosis (hardening of the arteries). High levels of LDL spell trouble for the heart.

There is a good type of cholesterol called High Density Lipoprotein, or HDL cholesterol. HDL cholesterol is good because it drags cholesterol back from the blood vessels into the liver, and out of harm's way.

There are also several other lesser known types of lipoprotein being studied to more accurately predict a person's level of risk. Higher levels of Very Low Density Lipoproteins (VLDL) and Intermediate Density Lipoproteins (IDL), and Lipoprotein-a, Lp(a), and apolipoprotein-B (apoB) are known to be bad news for the heart, as is C-Reactive protein (CRP), which is a marker for inflammation.

Summary of cholesterol types

LDL cholesterol—bad if high

HDL cholesterol—good if high

Triglycerides—bad if high

Other important blood fats

There are other fats in the blood called triglycerides, and these are a problem in excess as well as LDL cholesterol. Triglycerides are usually measured along with cholesterol in blood tests, and listed as 'TG'. High levels of triglycerides are converted to bad cholesterol in the liver, and are often elevated if you are overweight or have type 2 diabetes.

What do my blood test results mean?

To find out your cholesterol levels, your doctor will order a lipid profile blood test. Your blood levels will be listed on the left hand side of the page, and an ideal range or target level will be in brackets to the right. There can be small variability in the ranges and target

levels given by different testing laboratories, but your doctor will interpret your results for you.

Components of a lipid profile (cholesterol) blood test

- Total cholesterol
- Triglycerides
- LDL cholesterol
- HDL cholesterol
- Total cholesterol/HDL ratio
- LDL/HDL ratio

Except for HDL cholesterol, lower is better.

The total/HDL and LDL/HDL ratios, give you and your doctor an idea of the balance of power in your body between the bad cholesterol and the good HDL cholesterol. Lower ratio numbers are better because this reflects higher good HDL levels.

Cholesterol is measured in millimoles per litre of blood and abbreviated to mmol/L. A millimole is a chemical unit of measurement used in Australia, New Zealand and Europe.

In the USA, they use milligrams per decilitre, abbreviated to mg/dL.

What should my cholesterol be?

Except for HDL cholesterol, the lower your cholesterol level, the better.

More information in addition to a cholesterol level is needed to determine your absolute risk of heart disease. Talk to your GP.

Target cholesterol levels for those at increased risk

Total cholesterol	less than 4.0 mmol/L
*LDL cholesterol	less than 2.5 mmol/L
HDL cholesterol	greater than 1.0 mmol/L
Triglycerides	less than 1.5 mmol/L

* LDL levels are considered even more important than total cholesterol.

Total blood cholesterol level (US targets)

Desirable	less than 200 mg/dL
Borderline high risk	200-239 mg/dL
High risk	240 mg/dL and over

What makes cholesterol high?

There are a number of factors that can increase blood cholesterol levels. The most important factor is your family history. High cholesterol runs in families and you may be predisposed to high cholesterol because of your genes. Being male, and getting older also increase the likelihood of having high cholesterol

In terms of the factors within your control, diet is the most important. Eating too much saturated fat increases blood cholesterol. Eating too much cholesterol-rich foods can also make things worse, but it is a relatively small effect compared with the impact of a diet high in saturated fat. Eating unsaturated fats instead, and particularly polyunsaturated fats, lowers blood cholesterol.

Treatment of high cholesterol

Food versus drugs

A heart-healthy diet can produce similar cholesterol-lowering results to statin medications without the side effects and with added heart-health benefits. For example, statins can't lower blood pressure, cause weight and waist loss, lower homocysteine or blood glucose levels—all factors that can be influenced by diet. Prescribing guidelines for doctors in Australia require that patients receive dietary therapy for six weeks and then their lipid levels measured again before starting drugs. Our approach is optimal dietary therapy for lowering cholesterol levels.

Drugs to lower cholesterol

Healthy eating is important for everyone, whether you want to prevent high cholesterol and heart disease, or prevent it from getting worse once you have it. However, for people with very high cholesterol or at higher risk of CVD, medication is sometimes necessary alongside a heart-healthy lifestyle. There are four main drugs used to lower cholesterol: statins, fibrates, bile acid sequestrants and ezetimibe. They all come with potential risks and side effects, but are considered generally safe. Their effectiveness has been shown in clinical trials.

4: Avoiding heart break

The way to a man's heart is through his stomach. In the case of cholesterol and heart health, this can be taken literally! By helping him reduce the size of his stomach—making his waist measurement smaller—his heart will be healthier. And the same goes for women.

If you're above your ideal weight, losing weight will lower your cholesterol and reduce your risk of heart disease.

A day doesn't go by where we don't hear about the 'obesity epidemic'. We used to think that body fat just sat there and didn't do much but now we know that fat tissue (called adipose) is quite active, and in an undesirable way. Being overweight or obese

- increases cholesterol levels
- raises blood pressure
- increases the risk of type 2 diabetes
- increases the risk of heart disease

Carrying excess weight also creates inflammation in the body and inflammation is involved in hardening of the arteries, as well as many other chronic diseases.

Am I overweight?

Overweight is defined as having a body mass index (BMI) of 25 or higher. The BMI is a reliable indicator of body fat levels for most people, but it's a good idea to talk with your doctor or dietitian for a individual assessment.

Drawbacks of the BMI

The BMI does not accurately determine body fat levels in very muscle-bound sportspeople because it cannot distinguish whether the weight is fat or muscle. It's not that great for the elderly who have lost height and muscle either.

Some ethnic groups have different BMI classifications because they are heavier in build (eg Maori and Pacific Islanders), or they have more body fat at a lower weight (e.g. South East Asians). The BMI for overweight in Maori and Pacific Islanders is 26, and for 32 obesity.

How to work out your BMI

BMI = Weight (kg) ÷ Height in metres, squared (m2)
For example: If you weigh 85 kg and are 170 cm tall, your BMI is 85 divided by 1.7 squared (2.89), which is 29.

BMI rating scale and level of health risk (adult Europeans)

BMI	Classification	Risk of ill-health
18.5–24.9	Normal range	Average
25–29.9	Overweight	Increased
30–34.9	Obese I	Moderate
35–39.9	Obese II	Severe
Over 40	Obese III	Very severe

Body Mass Index (adult Asians)

Classification	BMI (kg/m2)	Risk of ill-health
Underweight	Less than 18.5	Low
Normal	18.5–22.9	Average
Overweight/Pre-obese	23–24.9	Increased
Obese class I	25–29.9	Moderate
Obese class II	Greater than 30	Severe

Waist matters

Where you store fat on your body is important for heart disease risk. Fat around the middle is bad news for the heart. This is often expressed in the simple terms 'apple-shaped' or 'pear-shaped', and apple-shaped people have the highest heart disease risk.

Measuring around your waist is a fairly reliable indicator of risky fat called central or abdominal obesity. If you have a higher waist than the targets in the table below, you have central obesity and it's time to take action for waist reduction. Another indicator of being apple-shaped is when your waist measurement is the same or more than your hip measurement.

In general, a healthy waistline is less than 80 cm for women and 94 cm for men.

How to measure your waist

It's best to have someone do this for you.
1. Take a tape measure and measure around the narrowest point, the level of your navel, or the midway point between your bottom rib and your (forward facing) hip bone (called the iliac crest).
2. Hold the tape snugly and measure after an out breath with a relaxed posture, with the arms by your side.

There's no use in measuring your waist if your BMI is 35 or above as you are automatically at very high risk.

Body fat scales

Bathroom scales are now available that can measure your percentage body fat through bio-impedance analysis. They work by passing a small electric current through your body and measuring the return current. These are not 100 per cent accurate, but close enough if you follow the instructions and weigh yourself at the same time of day each time. Although there are variations in recommended levels of body fat, acceptable levels for men are 8–25 per cent, and women 21–36 per cent.

Stop the spread!

We've all heard the expression 'middle-aged spread' and unfortunately surveys support the idea that the battle of the bulge is slowly lost as we get older. In Australia, being overweight increases with age and obesity is most common among those aged 55–64.

Preventing weight gain as we age is a vital heart-protection strategy. It is much more difficult to lose weight than to prevent weight gain in the first place. Weight gain causes cholesterol and triglyceride levels to rise, and often blood glucose and insulin levels as well. It can also bring problems of low self-esteem, low motivation and can make exercising more difficult (not to mention requiring a new wardrobe).

What's the right diet to lose weight?

There is no one diet that's right for everyone. There are many different ways to put together a nutritionally adequate weight loss diet. We all have different likes and dislikes, family food habits, meal routines and cooking skills so it's important that a weight loss diet suits you and your lifestyle so you can stick with it.

The key thing to remember is not how many fats, carbs or proteins there are, but the number of kilojoules you are eating and whether you're getting your quota of heart-friendly foods.

Extreme diets of any kind are not healthy. Let your common sense guide you towards moderation and avoid diets that eliminate or restrict whole food groups.

If you need some help to lose weight the best thing to do is make an appointment to see an Accredited Practising Dietitian (APD) or Registered Dietitian (RD) as they can tailor a weight loss eating plan to suit you and your lifestyle. Weight loss groups such as Weight Watchers can be helpful too if you need some support to stick with it.

The best way to lose weight is NOT on a low fat or low carb diet, but a nutritious and balanced LOW ENERGY (low-kilojoule) diet.

Energy explained

The 'energy' in food is another word for kilojoules or calories, so a 'high-energy' food can be a good or a bad thing depending on whether you're active enough to burn the energy during physical activity or exercise.

Remember, unused food energy can be stored as body fat and can cause weight gain. To work out how many kilojoules you need, see page 147 (part 3) for eating plans that are right for you.

Metabolism explained

You've probably heard people say that they can't lose weight because they have a slow metabolism.

The word 'metabolism' means how much energy (kilojoules) your body uses (or 'burns') each day to maintain itself. Our bodies constantly burn kilojoules to keep us going whether we are eating, sleeping, cleaning etc. Once the daily business of breathing, eating, moving and other activities are met, any unused or surplus calories get stored, mostly in the form of fat. This means that if you take in more kilojoules than you use, you will gain weight.

The speed at which your body burns those kilojoules is your metabolic rate. The higher your metabolic rate, the more food you need. The slower your metabolic rate, the greater the chance of weight gain

You can influence your metabolic rate by eating regularly, avoiding crash diets, increasing muscle and being physically active.

Weight gain is more likely to be due to an imbalance between food eaten and activity rather than a slow metabolism.

How much weight should I lose?

Just as there is no one diet to suit everyone, there is no right amount of weight to lose. For health benefits, losing just 5–10 per cent of your body weight makes a big difference to your heart disease risk factors such as cholesterol, blood pressure and blood glucose levels.

A realistic rate of weight loss is between 250 g–1 kg per week, with 1 kg per week being more appropriate for people starting at a higher weight.

Losing 1–4 cm from the waist per month in the short term with a 5 per cent reduction over a few months is a good goal.

It's perfectly normal (and in fact to be expected) to have weight loss plateaus. These occur because the body needs less energy at a lower weight. So think of the plateau as a sign post. To get off the plateau and continue to lose weight you need to do a little more (or a different type) of exercise and eat a little less food (kilojoules).

Even if you can't get down to the ideal BMI of less than 25 or your waist measurement into the target range, any weight or waist loss is beneficial. If you can't lose weight, preventing further weight gain is a good outcome for your heart.

Reassuring words

Some people are genetically programmed to be larger and the effort to slim down is unrealistic. If this is you, make the best of the cards you've been dealt and be as healthy as you can. Remember, healthy food and physical activity are protective for your heart.

You are better off being fat and enjoying a heart-healthy diet than being fat and eating badly.

The same goes for physical activity—you're better off being fat and fit, than a fat couch potato.

Thyroid alert

Having an under-active thyroid (hypothyroidism) slows the metabolism and makes weight loss very difficult, so have this checked by your doctor if you have been feeling particularly tired, lethargic, irritable, weak or if you have dry skin and hair, constipation or depression.

Forget low carb; go for low GI

The great news for those who love their carbs is that leading heart health organisations around the world say that the total amount of carbohydrate you eat has no association with developing cardiovascular disease; they encourage you to eat more heart-healthy whole-grains (see chapter 10 page 66).

Many wholegrain foods such as barley, traditional oats and grainy breads also have a low GI (glycemic index), which means they are slowly digested and absorbed into your bloodstream. This not only helps you control your blood glucose and insulin levels (vital if you have diabetes or pre-diabetes), but plays a useful role in your diet if you need to lose weight as these foods will keep you feeling fuller for longer.

What we now know is that being choosy about your carbs (foods like bread, rice, pasta, noodles, starchy vegetables and cereals) is just as important as being fussy about your fats. With carbs, the key is the rate of carbohydrate digestion. And here slow is better. Choosing quality carbs—the low GI ones that produce only small fluctuations in your blood glucose and insulin levels—is the secret to long-term health, reducing your risk of heart disease and diabetes and is the key to sustainable weight loss.

If you want to learn more about the glycemic index or check out the GI of your favourite carbohydrate foods, visit the University of Sydney's international GI website: www.glycemicindex.com.

Making the swap to lower GI carbs

Higher GI food	Lower GI alternative
White bread	Multigrain bread
Orange flavoured soft drink	Orange juice, unsweetened
Jelly beans	Dried apricots
Rice cracker	Rye crispbread
Corn flake cereal	Muesli
Puffed rice cereal	Traditional oat porridge

What is the glycemic index (GI)?

Just as there are good fats and bad fats, we now know that not all carbohydrate foods are created equal. The GI is a tool to help you control fluctuations in your blood glucose levels by choosing the smart low GI carbs.

Studies are showing that eating lots of high GI carbs tends to raise triglyceride levels. If you have high triglyceride levels, choosing low GI foods is especially important. A low GI diet appears to be protective against weight gain and heart disease and diabetes.

The GI itself is simply is a ranking of the immediate effect carbs have on your blood glucose levels. Carbs that break down quickly during digestion have a high GI and cause a rapid rise and decline in blood glucose. Carbs that break down slowly, releasing glucose gradually into your bloodstream have a low GI.

GI 55 or less is LOW
GI 56–69 is MEDIUM
GI 70 or more is HIGH

Forget fat-free, go for good fats

Low kilojoule diets are at risk of being low in nutrients unless you choose wisely. In the case of fats, you need to ensure you're choosing enough of the healthy fats to ensure you obtain adequate amounts of essential fatty acids (omega-3 and 6) and fat-soluble vitamins A, E and D. So it's out with the fatty meats, full cream dairy products, biscuits, cakes and pastries and in with the unsaturated vegetable oils and spreads, oily fish, nuts, seeds and avocado. You need at least 1½ tablespoons of healthy oils and spreads each day to get your quota and this amount is fine in a weight loss diet (see Eating plans to beat cholesterol on page 147).

Downsize portions

Portion sizes have increased dramatically over the years and this has added to our weight woes. We must get used to smaller portions (except for vegetables which we should eat more). In short, we must get used to eating less. You will find this difficult at first, however you will get used to being satisfied without needing to be stuffed full. Try using smaller sized plates, order an entrée sized meal at a restaurant, share a dessert or skip the bread basket.

Filling foods can help here as well, either through providing protein, or bulk (as in satisfying low GI carbs and vegetables). Get your protein satisfaction from lean meat, chicken or fish in your meals, and ensure you get your fill by ensuring you have plenty of vegetables or salad on your plate.

Retrain your appetite

To eat less and lose weight, some appetite re-training may be helpful. Many of us have tuned out from our natural hunger and satisfaction signals. This may be because we were taught as children to finish whatever is on our plate, we may be eating for emotional reasons, we may be in the habit of eating too quickly, or we're just generally stressed out and not fully 'present' when we eat. Being thirsty can masquerade as hunger as well so ensure you drink around two litres of fluid a day (that doesn't mean kilojoule-laden sweetened drinks). Water is the best drink.

A good way to tune back in to your natural signals is to keep a food, appetite and satisfaction diary. Remember, it's okay to overeat occasionally, just not regularly. It's ideal to be mostly 3s and 4s on the hunger and appetite scale.

Hunger and appetite scale
1 = uncomfortably full
2 = very full
3 = satisfied
4 = hungry
5 = very hungry
6 = Extremely hungry
Wait 10 minutes after finishing food before rating.

Fitting more into less

Cutting back on kilojoules to lose weight means you need to focus on nutritious foods to ensure your nutritional needs are met. This means eating more nutrient dense foods rather than energy dense and nutrient poor foods.

To do this you need to 'trim' extras from your diet and focus on heart-friendly foods such as vegetables, wholegrains, legumes, fruits, lean meats, low fat dairy foods, healthy oils, nuts and seeds. Of course, being physically active is also important. You may find you can eat a little more once you are active on a regular basis.

Examples of nutrient dense and energy dense, nutrient poor foods

Nutrient dense foods Eat more	Energy dense, nutrient poor foods Eat less
Vegetables and legumes	Soft drinks
Wholegrains	Cakes and biscuits
Fruits	Confectionary
Lean meats	Cream
Fish	Pastry
Nuts and seeds	Savoury packet snacks

What about treats?

Treats are fine, but remember, that's what they are—treats. That means occasional. In fact, in order to stick with a weight loss diet and not create cravings that may lead to binges, it is important to allow yourself to enjoy some treat foods. The trick is to limit the quantity and frequency to still allow you to lose weight. See the eating plans on page 155 for an idea of how many treat foods (and the serving size) you can fit into a reduced kilojoule eating plan. Of course, there are some people who stay right away from any treats, at least in the beginning stages of their weight loss diet.

Can I snack?

Choosing healthy snacks can be helpful for weight loss provided you're not eating more food than you need overall. Eating the same sized meals and adding snacks in—especially snacks high in kilojoules—and not being more active could actually result in weight gain. Having smaller meals and including nutritious foods between times can help control hunger and maintain more even blood glucose and energy levels.

Good snack choices are vegetables, fruit, wholegrain bread/crispbread, low fat milk and yoghurt, nuts and seeds. Some people benefit from snacks while others do best on three meals a day. Listen to your body to determine how you function better.

Diet traps

Being overweight or obese can make you vulnerable to quick-fix diets, pills and potions but if something sounds too good to be true, it usually is. You owe it to yourself to enjoy good health and a variety of nutritious foods without breaking the bank or going to extreme measures. If you have tried many diets before without long-term results, then these diets have failed you and a fresh approach is needed.

5: Two steps to beat cholesterol

It's your turn to take control of your cholesterol. In this chapter we set out the steps to lowering your cholesterol and protecting your heart.

Step 1: Move more

Increase your incidental activity by being active every day in as many ways as you can, such as taking the stairs rather than the lift or parking further away from the shops. We know you've heard it all before, but you really have to do it.

Find at least 30 minutes a day of moderate intensity physical activity such as walking or swimming. Doing more is even better.

If your doctor says it's okay, also do some vigorous activity such as running or aerobics. In the chapter 'Move more' we show you why being physically active can boost your health and wellbeing.

Step 2: Enjoy a heart-friendly diet

The heart-friendly diet harnesses the cholesterol-lowering abilities of heart-friendly foods. All these foods work in synergy to lower cholesterol, improve your heart health and optimise your wellbeing.

In Part 2 we take a closer look at these heart-friendly foods and highlight the really super foods that will make a significant difference to your cholesterol levels and heart health. Following are the dozen foods you need to incorporate into your diet.

1. Eat at least five serves of vegetables daily—a variety of colours and types including green, red/purple, yellow/orange and white.

Study after study has found vegetables are indeed nature's gifts for our health and longevity. The biggest vegetable eaters in the world also happen to be the healthiest. Vegetables are rich sources of valuable and heart-friendly nutrients such as vitamins, minerals, antioxidants and fibre, and all of this with few kilojoules attached. Enjoy at least five serves a day of a variety of colours and types to obtain your full quota of protection—and don't forget to enjoy them with a little healthy oil for great taste and to extract all their goodness. See page 38.

2. Enjoy at least two serves of fruit daily—a variety of types including citrus, berries and fruits like apples and pears.

A tenet of the famously healthy Mediterranean diet is 'no day without fruit' and this is great advice to really live by. Besides being deliciously sweet, refreshing and satisfying, fruit is packed full of protective vitamins and antioxidants as well as soluble fibre that lowers cholesterol. How can something that tastes so good be so good for you? Because this is the sweet treat nature intended for us to provide long lasting energy to burn. See page 50.

3. Boost natural food flavours with herbs and spices and reduce sodium (salt).

Herbs and spices are proof that healthy eating really is meant to be enjoyable. Not only do these kitchen essentials add flavour without salt, research is continually amazing us with their health benefits. Herbs and spices are where the natural flavour is, and flavour means fun to eat. Have them on hand to turn basic heart-friendly ingredients into gastronomic experiences that taste good and are good for you. See page 61.

4. Ensure half your grain foods are wholegrains (at least two serves daily, such as two slices of wholemeal bread and a bowl of wholegrain cereal).

Wholegrains are a classic case of 'what is old is new again'. We've now realised that processing our grains makes them less nutritious and if we leave them be they can deliver a hefty dose of heart protection. Wholegrains are those with the bran and germ present, such as wholemeal bread or rolled oats, while refined grains have the bran polished away such as white rice and white flour. We need to 'bring back the brown' in the form of wholegrain breads and cereals. Enjoy at least half your daily grain foods as wholegrain versions (two serves a day, such as ½ cup of brown rice and a ⅔ cup of porridge) to lower cholesterol and keep heart attacks at bay. See page 66.

5. Include low GI foods at most meals.

Low GI carbohydrate foods help you control your blood glucose levels throughout the day, which means more stable energy levels, happy and relaxed blood vessels and a healthy heart. GI values are simply a numerical ranking as compared with glucose which has a GI of 100. Carbs that break down quickly during digestion have high GI values; carbs that break down slowly releasing glucose gradually into the bloodstream have low GI values. There are plenty of wholesome heart-friendly low GI foods to choose from, such as multigrain bread, pasta, barley, sweetcorn, high-fibre breakfast cereals, muesli, porridge, most fruits, legumes, soy milk, low fat milk and yoghurt. You'll find lower GI recipes highlighted in part 3. You can check the GI of a food using the database at www.glycemicindex.com.

6. Include legumes such as beans, chickpeas or lentils in at least two meals per week (more is better).

Legumes such as kidney beans, baked beans, chickpeas and lentils are a cornerstone of the famously healthy Mediterranean diet. They are super-healthy with stacks of plant protein, cholesterol lowering soluble-fibre, vitamins, minerals and antioxidants. And they have a low GI. Naturally low in fat, cheap and highly versatile in cooking, make legumes your friends and include them in at least two meals a week to reap the heart-health benefits. Don't forget, the canned varieties save time in the kitchen—convenience plus! See page 74.

7. Enjoy 30 g/1 oz (1 small handful) of nuts most days.

Forget every bad thing you've heard about nuts! They're highly nutritious and packed full of heart-friendly nutrients such as unsaturated fats, plant protein, minerals, fibre and antioxidants. Enjoying 30 g (1 small handful) of nuts a day has been shown to reduce the risk of heart disease, so enjoy them daily either on their own or as part of a meal. Seeds are the nutrition powerhouse to grow a whole new plant and are great for you too. Nuts and seeds add flavour and texture and really dress up a stir fry, salad, breakfast or dessert. See page 81.

8. Enjoy fish in at least two meals a week (preferably oily fish).

Fish, particularly oily fish, are true heart-friendly foods and this has been shown time and time again in scientific studies. The protective component is long chain omega-3 polyunsaturated fats, among others. These biologically active fats have the ability to dramatically reduce the risk of death from heart attack by thinning the blood and preventing clots as well as ensuring a smooth and regular heart beat. Enjoy at least two fish meals—preferably oily fish—per week and keep an eye out for foods with added omega-3 to ensure your omega-3 levels are topped up. See page 90.

9. Enjoy at least 1½ tablespoons of healthy oils and spreads daily.

Getting your fats right is step 1 of a cholesterol lowering eating pattern. The golden rule is to get rid of saturated fats and replace them with healthy unsaturated fats—both mono- and polyunsaturated—ensuring you include essential omega-3 and -6 polyunsaturates the body cannot make and must obtain from food. You can obtain healthy unsaturated fats in nuts, seeds, fish and even wholegrains, but the best sources are the oils you use in cooking and the spread you use on your bread. Good oils include canola, olive, mustard seed, macadamia nut, peanut, rice bran, safflower, sesame, sunflower, soybean and walnut oils and spreads made from these. You need at least 1 ½ tablespoons a day of oils and spreads to achieve a healthy balance—this amount is healthy even if you need to lose weight (see page 20 for weight loss information).

10. Eat 25 g of plant sterol-enriched spread (1 rounded tablespoon) daily as part of your daily healthy oil target.

Plant sterols are naturally occurring substances found in vegetable oils, nuts, seeds and grains that reduce cholesterol absorption from the gut and lower bad LDL cholesterol. Plant sterol-enriched spreads have been convincingly shown to lower blood cholesterol in scientific studies. Use 25 g a day (one rounded table-spoon) on bread, sandwiches, toast, in baking, or melted into vegetables to lower your cholesterol by an average of 10 per cent! See page 106.

11. If you choose to drink alcohol, enjoy one or two standard drinks daily.

Alcohol in moderation appears to be protective for the heart, especially if you're middle aged or older. This is not to say you should take up drinking if you don't drink currently, but if you do enjoy a tipple you can feel good about enjoying one or two drinks a day. The other good news? It doesn't matter what type of alcohol. Whether it is wine, beer or sprits you enjoy, they're all good for the heart. See also page 122.

12. If you drink tea and coffee, enjoy in moderation (up to three or four teas plus two or three instant coffees—or one strong coffee—daily).

These reviving beverages are a source of essential fluids as well as protective antioxidants that help look after the heart and blood vessels. Tea and coffee are social drinks that help bring us together and help us to take 'time-out' for ourselves. Enjoyed in moderation and without the addition of full cream milk and too much sugar, tea and coffee can be part of a heart-healthy eating pattern. See page 129.

6: Move more

There's no getting around it, if you want to say goodbye to cholesterol, you've got to get active. Your body was made to move. Today most of us have to make a conscious effort to set aside special times to be active whether it's taking a walk or working out in the gym or having a game of netball or tennis or touch footy.

What's so good about physical activity?

Being active reduces your risk of developing heart disease, as well as other diseases such as type 2 diabetes, osteoporosis, obesity, depression and cancer. Even moderate improvements in your fitness levels can deliver substantial health benefits. If you already have heart disease, being physically active can:

- decrease bad cholesterol levels
- increase good cholesterol levels
- improve blood flow
- increase your heart's ability to do its job—pumping the blood around your body

It is NEVER too late to fit physical activity into your lifestyle!

What is resistance training and why is it important?

Doing some low to moderate resistance (strength) training improves muscular strength and endurance. Being physically stronger helps you to walk tall and get things done. Resistance training is a method of conditioning muscles, joints and bones which involves the progressive use of resistance to increase your ability to exert force. Lifting weights is an example, but body weight can also be used such as doing a push-up.

Regular physical activity produces a number of favourable changes to your heart and blood vessels.

The heart's ability to pump blood around your body is improved (better functional capacity). Being more active boosts mood, reduces the risk of blood clots (thrombosis), keeps the heart beating smoothly and regularly (reduces risk of arrhythmia), increases the amount of oxygen transported throughout the body and reduces the risk of atherosclerosis (hardening of the arteries).

What's the difference between exercise and incidental physical activity?

Whether its incidental physical activity or exercise you do, any way you get moving is worthwhile. Including more incidental activity in your day adds up over the year and is beneficial. Structured exercise provides you with additional health benefits.

Physical activity is any bodily movement produced by your muscles which results in expending energy beyond what you would expend at a resting level. For instance doing the ironing or washing your car are both classified as physical activity.

Exercise is physical activity which you plan to include in your day for leisure, recreation or fitness. It has a planned purpose such as improving fitness, performance, health or as a social activity. For example, swimming or going for your daily 'constitutional' walk.

Different types of activity
Incidental physical activity

Incidental activity is the kind that has gone backwards as technology has moved forwards. To increase your incidental activity, be active every day in as many ways as you can!

For example
- Taking the stairs instead of the lift
- Ironing
- Gardening
- Doing housework
- Parking further away from the shops and walking
- Walking to the train station
- Getting off your bus or train a stop early
- Getting up to change the television channel instead of using the remote control
- Get up, stretch and walk around at work
- Walk or play with pets
- Play with children in an active way

Tip

Get yourself a pedometer—a little gadget you wear on your belt to keep track of how many steps you take do each day. Establish your usual number (baseline), and then set small increases week by week. A good target is 10 000 steps a day—but you may want to start with 7500.

Moderate intensity exercise

Remember that structured exercise provides you with additional health benefits, so set aside 30 minutes each day to go for a walk, a swim or a ride.

For example

- Aquarobics (water aerobics)
- Brisk walking
- Cycling
- Yoga
- Swimming
- Golf
- Line dancing
- Resistance training

Vigorous activity

If you are able to, vigorous activity has even more benefits. However, vigorous activity is not routinely recommended for people with existing heart disease. Check with your doctor first.

For example

- Running
- Netball or basketball
- Soccer
- Rugby or touch rugby or AFL
- Tennis or squash
- Uphill walking
- Aerobics
- Circuit training
- Rowing

Levels of intensity of physical activity

Low intensity physical activity—movement that slightly increases your breathing rate e.g. strolling on level firm ground or social lawn bowls.

Moderate intensity physical activity—movement that moderately and noticeable increases your depth and breathing rate, while still allowing you to comfortably talk e.g. cycling for pleasure or cleaning the house.

Vigorous intensity physical activity—movement at a higher intensity, which depending on fitness level, may cause sweating and puffing.

How much should you do?

Australia's National Physical Activity Guidelines for Adults recommend including at least 30 minutes of moderate intensity physical activity on most, preferably all days of the week. If you have high cholesterol levels, these physical activity guidelines are even more important for you. For children, the recommendation is at least 60 minutes a day of moderate activity, and some vigorous activity is recommended.

The 30 minutes is a minimum amount. You get even more health benefits from longer periods. Thankfully for busy people and the very unfit, these 30 minutes don't have to be continuous. You can put together the 30 minutes in short bouts. For example, you could go for a 15 minute walk in the morning and then a 15 minute swim in the afternoon, or do three 10 minute walks a day.

The benefits of being active outweigh the risks

The most common risk associated with physical activity in general is hurting yourself (musculoskeletal injury), but this risk can be reduced if you increase your physical activity gradually over time. If you enjoy walking, gardening or cycling, the chance of injury is low.

Special care is needed if you have heart disease already. Vigorous activity is not usually recommended and the risk of sudden death is increased. If you're still keen, you need to have medical screening and assessment first. Moderate activity is much safer.

If you're doing little or nothing now, the thought of starting might seem daunting. A change of thinking can help. Rather than thinking of physical activity as a punishment or inconvenience, think of it as an opportunity to feel better. Remember, your body was made to move. Start off slowly and realistically. Simple choices such as walking to pick up the morning paper rather than driving can make a big difference over the long term.

Tip 1: Build up gradually

Australia's National Heart Foundation supports these physical activity recommendations, but suggests that if you already have cardiovascular disease, this physical activity should be built up gradually over time. The word gradually should be taken seriously. Changing from a couch potato to a fitness fanatic overnight is heart attack material.

Tip 2: Before you start see your GP

If you are sedentary, you need to see your GP for a pre-activity evaluation. This evaluation should include medications review, medical review, physical examination and a history of your physical activity. Once you get the all clear from your GP, it is recommended that you gradually build up your activity levels from that of low intensity to the recommended dose (30 minutes moderate) of physical activity.

Tip 3: Get expert advice

It's best that the level of physical activity you do is tailored to meet your needs and capacity, and take into account any disease process, reduced function or poor balance. The best people to do this are exercise physiologists or physiotherapists.

Tip 4: Warm up and down to reduce the risk of muscle soreness

To reduce the risk of developing muscle soreness or injuries, remember to always warm-up before and cool-down after your exercise session. This means you need to start off slowly before increasing the pace, and then slow down gradually at the end rather than start off racing and come to an abrupt halt. Your muscles will thank you.

Warm-up

Five to ten minutes in duration: Begin with gentle stretches focusing on warming up the muscles that you plan to use in the exercise session—e.g. if you're going to ride your bike, stretch your legs and then cycle at a slower pace than normal for a few minutes.

Cool-down

Five to ten minutes in duration: Gradually slow down your exercise pace and then stretch the muscles you used.

Tip 5: Be SMART. Set goals

In order to be more active and improve your health and wellbeing, it's important that you set goals. Personal goals will help motivate you to change and give you something to work towards. Your goals should be clear and achievable, because unrealistic goals set you up for disappointment. Ensure your goals are SMART.

SMART Goals
S—Specific
M—Measurable
A—Achievable
R—Realistic
T—Time-bound

A SMART goal example
'We will attend three afternoon aquarobic sessions each week for the next month.'

Being active is something you want to keep doing for the rest of your life, so there's no need to rush into things. By setting yourself a monthly goal, you are making the small steps needed to build larger, longer term goals. The success of achieving goals is a great motivator.

Tip 6: Keep a Workout Diary

A good way to keep track of physical activity is to keep a Workout Diary. By recording the duration, type and intensity of activity each day, you can easily see how far you have come. The Workout Diary will help you to monitor whether you are achieving your goals, and will also assist you in re-establishing any goals that may be unrealistic. Remember if your goal was to walk for 30 minutes on five days a week for the next month and you have done this easily for the last 2 months, you've definitely achieved your goal and probably need to develop another one. Remember the more you do the better, and variety of physical activity keeps your body working in different ways and prevents boredom.

You've made a great start, how do you stay motivated to continue it for the long term?

- Don't rush into things. Set realistic goals that you know are achievable.
- Listen to your body to decide if it's time to step up your amount of activity or if it's time to rest.
- Schedule physical activities in your diary like other appointments.
- Ask your friends, family or work colleagues to get active with you.

Part 2

Say hello
to heart-friendly foods

7: Vegetables

Vegetables are low in kilojoules but high in filling power and nutritional goodness, making them great to eat when you're watching your weight and getting your cholesterol down. Eating vegetables reduces risk of cardivascular disease and reduces your chances of becoming overweight and developing some cancers.

Vegetables are nature's very own functional foods—full of essential nutrients such as vitamins, minerals and fibre, as well as protective phytochemicals such as antioxidants. And it's never too late to start getting the veggie benefit. So pile them on your plate.

When it comes to vegetables, it's not just 'your greens' you need to eat. Let colour be your guide and aim to serve at least three different coloured veggies on the dinner plate each day. It looks good. And it is good. Colour is a useful indicator of a vegetable's protective phytochemical content. Carrots, for example, are orange because they are high in beta-carotene—a powerful antioxidant—as are sweet potatoes and pumpkin.

Are you getting enough?

The more the better! It's impossible to overdose on veggies. However, most health experts recommend five servings a day as a good target to aim for. A serving is around a handful, so try to get five handfuls of vegetables into your day.

What is a serve?

- ½ cup cooked vegetables or legumes (about 75 g/2½ oz)
- a medium sized potato (about 150 g/5 oz)
- a cup of salad vegetables (enough to fill a small dessert bowl)
- a medium sized tomato (about 100 g/3½ oz)
- a small carrot (about 100 g/3½ oz)
- ½ cup of sweet potato chunks (about 70 g/2½ oz)
- ¾ cup (180 ml/6 fl oz) of vegetable juice
- a cup (250 ml/9 fl oz) of vegetable soup

What are phytochemicals?

'Phyto' means plant, so phytochemicals are plant chemicals. They're naturally occurring defenders of your health, rather like your body's security guards keeping out troublemakers like free radicals. Antioxidants are phytochemicals. But there's literally a whole army of them in the food we eat, particularly in plant foods such as vegetables, fruits, wholegrains, nuts and seeds.

What are antioxidants?

Antioxidants protect your body from damage caused by free radicals. Free radicals promote oxidation—a process similar to metal rusting. Oxidative damage by free radicals is thought to contribute to diseases like heart disease and even the ageing process. Although free radicals are formed in your body's normal biochemical processes, their formation increases during inflammation, exposure to sun, pollution like smog and cigarette smoke (your own or someone else's). Eating foods rich in protective antioxidants can reduce the damage caused by free radicals. So if you want to stay protected, 'rust-proof' your body with plenty of antioxidant-rich plant foods.

Is fresh best?

Raw or cooked?

Whole or juiced?

Fresh or frozen?

What's the best way to get the goodness of vegetables? Any way you can! However you enjoy your veggies—raw, cooked or juiced—it will contribute to your five servings a day. There's no need to embark on a raw food diet. While cooking reduces some nutrients and phytochemicals a little, it makes others easier to absorb. So enjoy a combination of both raw and cooked vegetables, depending on what you feel like. The fresh crunch of a crisp and cool salad is perfect for a hot summer evening by the barbecue, but nothing beats baked vegetables with a roast dinner on a chilly winter's night. Veggie soups are great, too. Cool down with a chilled soup like gazpacho; or warm up with a satisfying minestrone.

To preserve the nutritional goodness of vegetables, the best cooking methods are baking, microwaving, steaming and stir-frying. Avoid boiling as you will be pouring the vitamins down the drain with the cooking water.

There's nothing wrong with opting for convenience when it comes to buying vegetables. Choosing frozen and canned vegetables occasionally enables you to enjoy a wide variety of vegetables year round.

Frozen vegetables are picked and snap frozen at their peak which makes them a nutritious option. In fact frozen peas retain more of their vitamins than shelled pre-packed peas on the greengrocer's shelf.

Canned vegetables such as tomatoes, legumes and corn help you to prepare nutritious meals in minutes. Choose salt-reduced options where possible, or drain well—most salt is in the liquid

Vegetable juices such as tomato, carrot and mixed juices help you achieve your five servings of veggies a day and provide a healthy alternative to soft drinks and cordials. The downside is the fibre lost during the juicing process.

Stressed out? Tired? Run down? Boost your vitality with a phyto-power pick-me-up of freshly squeezed carrot, celery and ginger juice.

How to get your 'five vegetables a day'

Breakfast

• Make a hearty beginning with wholegrain toast, grilled tomatoes, sautéed mushrooms and a poached egg on a bed of sautéed spinach or silverbeet (swiss chard).

• Start the day with zing with tomato juice and a dash of tabasco.

• Fill a small omelette with sautéed onion, capsicum, mushrooms, sprouts and baby spinach leaves.

• Use leftover rice to make an Asian rice porridge, or congee, with salt-reduced vegetable stock and Asian greens such as bok choy, pak choy or tai soi.

Lunch

• Take a salad to work. What about baby spinach leaves, cherry tomatoes, cucumber slices, blanched green beans, walnuts and avocado with a citrus and olive oil dressing.

• Have leftovers for lunch, heated up, or transformed into a soup with salt-reduced stock or pureed canned tomatoes, or a vegetable frittata with beaten egg and a little low fat ricotta.

Dinner

• Warm up to your main meal with a vegetable soup.

• Complement main meals with salad.

• Pile up your dinner plate with vegetables—with at least three different coloured veggies.

• Make-over your favourite recipes by adding extra vegetables.

• With takeaways, stretch the meal and boost nutrition with extra veggies. Serve barbecue chicken with baby potatoes, a cob of corn and an endive, tomato and zucchini salad; partner pizza with a garden salad; accompany curries with extra veggies such as cucumber or carrot raitas.

Snacks

• Crunch on a sweet and juicy cob of corn.

• Nibble on juicy cherry tomatoes.

• Dunk crisp vegetable sticks of carrot, celery, capsicum and snowpeas into hummus or cucumber dips.

• Dip spicy homemade pita crisps into low fat eggplant dip or capsicum and corn or tomato salsa.

Don't let your vegetables go naked! Quick dressings for 2

Dress up your vegetables and salads with healthy oils like canola, sunflower, olive, sesame, grapeseed or mustardseed, mixed with vinegar or lemon juice, herbs, spices or mustard.

Vinaigrette

Place 3 teaspoons olive oil, 1 teaspoon lemon juice or white wine vinegar and ¼ teaspoon wholegrain mustard in a screw-top jar. Shake to combine, taste and season with sugar and freshly ground black pepper. Add some freshly chopped or dried herbs, such as parsley, basil or dill for a herb vinaigrette.

Chilli and Lime Dressing

Place 2 teaspoons extra light olive or peanut oil, 1 teaspoon sesame oil, ½ teaspoon salt-reduced soy sauce, 2 teaspoons sweet chilli sauce, 1 teaspoon lime juice and some freshly chopped herbs, such as Vietnamese mint, coriander or Thai basil in a screw-top jar. Shake to combine, taste and adjust flavours to suit.

Citrus Dressing

Place 1 tablespoon freshly squeezed orange juice, 1 teaspoon freshly squeezed lemon or lime juice and 2 teaspoons olive or sunflower oil in a screw-top jar. Shake to combine, taste and adjust flavour to suit, adding a little sugar for sweetness if liked.

Green vegetables
What are they?

Look for leafy greens or green skinned vegetables (that you eat the skin of) such as:

Artichoke

Asparagus

Beans

Broccoli

Broccolini

Brussels sprouts

Bok choy or baby bok choy

Cabbage

Capsicum

Celery

Chicory (curly endive)

Chilli, green

Choy sum, baby choy sum

Cress

Endive, curly endive

English spinach, baby English spinach

Gai lan (Chinese broccoli)

Gai choy

Kale

Kang kong

Lamb's lettuce (mâche)

Lettuce including crisphead (iceberg), cos (romaine), butterhead, and loose leaf (mignonette, oak, coral and salad mixes such as mesclun)

Lebanese cucumber

Mizuna

Mustard greens (Daai gaai choi)

Okra

Pak choy (or baby pak choy)

Peas

Rocket (arugula)

Silverbeet (Swiss chard)

Snowpeas (mangetout)

Sugar snap peas

Spring onions

Spinach

Spring onions (shallots)

Sprouts including alfalfa, mung beans and wheatgrass

Sugarsnap peas

Tai soi

Watercress

Witlof (Belgian endive)

Zucchini (courgette)

Why vegetables are good for you

Green vegetables are rich in antioxidants and folate. The darker their green colour, the more they contain which is why broccoli and Asian greens are so good for you. Greens are also packed with fibre, potassium, magnesium, calcium and a little iron. Vegetables from the cabbage (cruciferous) family such as broccoli, cabbage, cauliflower and Brussels sprouts also contain special kinds of phytochemicals called indoles and isothiocyanates. Aim for a minimum of three cups of green vegetables a week for good health.

TIPS FOR GREENS

- Always have one green vegetable on your dinner plate.
- Choose darker coloured lettuces for their higher levels of antioxidants.
- Cook greens quickly (steaming or stir frying), or add at the end of cooking time to preserve their nutrient content.
- Eat greens in season and they'll be at their nutritional peak, and cheaper.
- Eat green vegetables the day you buy them if possible or store in a plastic bag in the fridge crisper to keep them fresher for longer.

One of the reasons that vegetables and fruit 'rot' in your fridge is because they emit ethylene gas. You can now buy special storage bags and cartridges (Keepfresh) for the crisper that absorb ethylene and slow down the ageing and ripening process.

What about fresh herbs?

Give salads and sandwiches a flavour boost with basil, parsley, mint, chives or coriander. Green leafy herbs are similar in nutritional content to green vegetables. They also add fantastic flavour, but it is more delicate than dried herbs so add at the end of cooking time. To store, wrap them in paper towel and place in a plastic bag in the fridge so they last longer, or stand them up in a jar of water in the refrigerator with a plastic bag over the top.

How to get more

- Pile coloured lettuce, rocket or baby spinach onto a chicken or tuna and tomato sandwich.
- Add Asian greens such as bok choy, gai choy or gai lan to beef, seafood and chicken stir-fries, noodle soups and broths.
- Make a complete meal salad with a variety of lettuces and witlof, shredded chicken and salad vegetables.
- Add steamed and then cooled broccoli or broccolini to a green salad with radishes and serve with steamed white fish, a drizzle of extra virgin olive oil and toasted flaked almonds.
- Sauté lean pork strips and cabbage, brussels sprouts or kale in some canola oil with finely sliced onion and a little sugar, dress with vinegar and serve with mashed potato and carrots.
- Make coleslaw with shredded green (and red) cabbage or wombok, carrot, kohlrabi, coriander and peanuts. Stir in some shaved (or chopped) low fat deli ham and roll in wholemeal flat bread.
- Use frozen spinach in lean beef or vegetable lasagna, filo ham and ricotta pastries, beef and chicken soups, vegetable omelettes and frittatas.
- Broccoli, beans and snow peas (mangetout) or sugar snap peas are delicious cold in a red kidney bean and onion salad.
- Add fresh or frozen peas to tuna pasta, chicken rice or roasted vegetable couscous dishes and chicken noodle soups.

Quickie for 2

Broccoli and Green Bean Salad

Served either at room temperature or chilled this salad can be the perfect partner to turn barbecued meat, seafood or vegetables into a Mediterranean or Asian-style meal—try the different dressing suggestions. Add a noodle or brown rice salad to complete the meal.

Steam or microwave 2 cups small broccoli florets and 1 cup sliced green beans until the colour has intensified yet, the vegetables are still crisp (al dente). Refresh and cool in cold water and drain. Combine with a of clove of crushed garlic a tablespoon of vinaigrette dressing or opt for an Asian flavour and toss in 1 tablespoon salt-reduced soy sauce or kecap manis and 1 tablespoon toasted sesame seeds.

TIPS FOR COOKING GREENS

Cooked cruciferous vegetables such as Asian greens, Brussels sprouts and cabbage don't taste as good the next day because their bitter flavours become more pronounced. Cook just enough for the meal, and cook lightly to keep the flavour just right.

Red and purple vegetables
What are they?

Look for leafy red/purple vegetables or red/purple skinned vegetables (which you eat the skin of) such as:

Basil, purple

Beetroot

Cabbage, red

Capsicum, red

Cauliflower, purple

Chilli, red

Eggplant (aubergine)

Endive, purple

Lettuce, red including oak leaf and mignonette

Radicchio

Radishes

Red onion (Spanish)

Rhubarb

Sweet potato, red (kumara)

Tomatoes

Why they are good for you

Red and purple vegetables are rich in antioxidants such as anthocyanins, phenolics and carotenoids. Tomatoes contain a particular carotenoid antioxidant called lycopene. Like all vegetables, they also contain vitamins such as C, and minerals such as potassium.

How to get more

- Grill halved Roma tomatoes with a drop of olive oil and balsamic vinegar. Enjoy them hot with a cooked breakfast, or cool them down and add to salads or sandwiches.

- Roast red capsicum in a hot oven until the skin blackens. Place immediately into a plastic bag until cool and then remove the skin (which should slide off easily). Slice or dice and enjoy as a side dish with grilled meat or seafood and salad, in a warm beef, oak leaf lettuce and Asian herb salad, or added to pasta or sandwiches.

- Add thin red (Spanish) onion rings to Asian-style salads, or chop finely and add to a salmon sandwich with mignonette lettuce (or purple endive) and tomato, or sardines on toast with baby greens tossed in lemon juice.

- Add purple basil to meat and vegetable stir-fries, or add to a green salad of cos lettuce, asparagus and snow (or sugar snap) peas for flavour and colour.

- Quick-roast slices, chunks or pieces of capsicum, red onion, red sweet potato (kumara) and beetroot by microwaving first until tender.

- Make a quick beetroot dip with chopped canned (drained) beetroot and low fat natural yoghurt and a clove of crushed garlic. Great with vegetable sticks and wholemeal pita bread triangles.

- Lightly steam or microwave purple asparagus, drizzle with extra virgin olive oil and lemon juice and zest and add to a chicken, avocado and watercress salad.

Quickie for 2

Ratatouille

This basic vegetable sauce is jam packed with colours and flavours and can be served as a topping with pasta, steamed vegetables, meats or toast, or added to a sandwich or roll for delicious Mediterranean flavour.

Heat a tablespoon olive oil and cook 1 small sliced brown onion and a crushed clove of garlic until soft (about 5 minutes). Add half a diced small eggplant and cook until golden (2 minutes). Add 1 small sliced zucchini, 1 sliced small red capsicum (pepper) and stir for 2 minutes. Add 1 cup diced canned tomatoes, a teaspoon sugar and a tablespoon each of red wine vinegar and white wine. Stir well, cover and gently simmer for about 30 minutes. Serve immediately or refrigerate and use as required. Makes about 2 cups.

- Brush eggplant slices with olive oil, grill on the barbecue until tender and serve as part of a mezze platter or an antipasto plate.

- Stew rhubarb and apple until tender, add sugar and lemon juice to taste and serve as a condiment with white meats.

- Blanch cauliflower, purple or white, florets and toss through salads.

- Serve a small dish of sliced red chilli on the side of any Asian-style dishes.

Did you know?

The antioxidants in tomatoes are better absorbed when they are cooked with a little oil–enter pasta sauce! Homemade or ready-prepared, pasta sauce is a nutritious way to enjoy not only pasta but vegetables and lean meats as well. Traditional Italian cooks serve thick and rich tomato sauces with meat, fish, vegetables and legumes to add flavour.

Orange and yellow vegetables
What are they?

Look for orange- or yellow-fleshed vegetables or with orange/yellow skin (which you eat the skin of) such as:

Beans, yellow

Butternut squash

Capsicum (pepper), yellow

Carrots

Pumpkin

Sweet corn, baby corn

Sweet potato (kumara)

Tomatoes, yellow

Yellow squash

Yellow zucchini (courgette)

Why they are good for you

Yellow and orange vegetables contain antioxidants called carotenoids (e.g. beta-carotene) and flavonoids, as well as the usual vegetable nutrient goodies like vitamin C and fibre. The orange coloured beta-carotene is converted to vitamin A in the body. Vitamin A is important for healthy vision.

How to get more

- Microwave chunks of pumpkin until tender. Lightly spray with olive oil before baking until cooked and golden. Use in roasted pumpkin and tomato soup or roasted pumpkin, coriander and cumin rice with an Indian spiced beef stew.
- Snack on sweet baby carrots or cooked and cooled baby corn.
- Add grated carrot to sandwiches, mince and egg dishes or try a grated carrot, grated daikon (white radish) and grated green apple for a crunchy garnish to any Asian-style meal.
- Serve creamed corn on toast for a healthy hot breakfast.
- Barbecue or microwave corn on the cob in its husk and enjoy a delicious entrée.
- Thread cubes of yellow, green and orange capsicum and quartered baby yellow squash onto skewers with cubes of lean meat or chicken and grill or barbecue for colourful kebabs.
- Make a peanut butter, grated carrot and raisin sandwich on multigrain bread.
- Halved yellow tomatoes and sliced yellow zucchinis make a colourful addition to a tuna, beetroot, cos lettuce and walnut salad.
- Butternut squash mash is a great alternative to potato mash and great with grilled fish.

Quickies for 2

Sweet Potato Wedges

Perfect for a snack or for a quick roast or a barbecue accompaniment. Roast or barbecue chicken, fish or meat and the wedges. Serve with couscous and a leafy green salad.

Preheat an oven to moderately hot 200°C (400°F/Gas mark 6). Blend 3 teaspoons extra light olive oil, ½ teaspoon ground sweet paprika and ¼ teaspoon ground cumin in a bowl. Add 2 cups peeled sweet potato wedges and mix to coat wedges. Spray a baking tray with olive oil spray and place wedges, in one layer, on the tray. Bake for 20 minutes or until cooked, turning once during cooking or cook in a disposable dish on a covered barbecue.

Spiced Stuffed Yellow Capsicum

Makes a great light lunch followed by citrus fruit.

Heat 2 teaspoons canola or peanut oil and cook 1 teaspoon garam masala for 1 minute. Add ¾ cup drained four bean mix, ¾ cup canned chopped (no added salt) tomatoes, cover and simmer on low heat for 10 minutes. Stir in ½ cup wholemeal or mixed grain breadcrumbs (look for the lowest sodium bread) and heat. Cut a yellow capsicum (pepper) in half lengthways, remove the seeds and steam or microwave until tender. Fill each half of the capsicum with bean mixture and sprinkle with about a tablespoon of freshly chopped coriander.

White vegetables
What are they?

Look for white or creamy skinned or fleshed vegetables such as:

Avocado
Cauliflower
Celeriac
Daikon
Fennel
Garlic
Ginger
Kohlrabi
Leeks
Mushrooms
Onions
Parsnips
Potatoes
Shallots
Swedes
Taro
Turnip
Yams

Why they are good for you

Onions, leeks and garlic contain a phytochemical called allicin as well as flavonols and sulfur compounds thought to have cancer-protective effects. Swedes and turnips are rich in a group of phytochemical called glucosinolates. Root vegetables all contain vitamin C and are a good source of fibre.

Quickies for 2

Garlic Mayonnaise (Aioli)

If you struggle to eat enough vegetables, try them with a spoon of this delicious garlic mayonnaise (aioli) that combines healthy oils with the health-boosting effects of garlic.

Mix 2 cloves crushed garlic and 1 teaspoon lemon juice into 1½ tablespoons canola or soy bean oil mayonnaise.

Cauliflower, Pea and Potato Curry

Enjoy this recipe with steamed brown rice and a microwaved pappadum.

Heat 1 tablespoon canola oil with 1 or 2 teaspoons curry powder, add 1 cubed coliban potato and cook, stirring, for about 5 minutes. Add 3 cups cauliflower florets, 1 cup canned (no added salt) diced tomatoes and ½ cup water. Cover and simmer on low for 10 minutes, stirring occasionally to prevent sticking. Stir in a cup each of drained canned chickpeas and frozen peas and cook for about 1 or 2 minutes until peas are cooked. Top with diced tomato, low fat plain yoghurt and chopped coriander.

How to get more

- Try different styles of mash such as parsnip and potato with chopped onion; swede, potato and roasted garlic; potato and celeriac or yam with chopped chives. Serve with a juicy lean steak and a green leaf, tomato, shallot and mushroom salad.
- Cook cauliflower and broccoli florets and carrot sticks in the microwave until tender and then sauté briefly in some olive oil and crushed garlic. Sprinkle with toasted sesame seeds and serve as a warm salad mixed with pan-fried lean beef strips.
- Make taro and parsnip chips with slivers made with a vegetable peeler, and then deep fry in canola oil until crisp and golden. Add them to a chicken Caesar salad to replace the croutons. High kilojoule alert! Go easy if you're watching your weight.
- Slice a whole head of unpeeled garlic across the centre with a sharp knife and roast or barbecue. Serve as is; the soft and sweet flesh can be scooped out and enjoyed as a condiment for grilled or barbecue meats or seafood.
- Sauté leeks and mushrooms in olive oil with a little smoked paprika and serve as a toast topping, or add diced chicken for a pasta sauce
- Add chopped ginger and thinly sliced kohlrabi to Asian tofu and vegetable stir-fry, or add crushed ginger to boiling water with a little honey for ginger tea

- Finely chop shallots and mix with chopped tomato, garlic and a little balsamic vinegar—perfect on poached chicken or fish with a fennel, avocado and lamb's lettuce (mâche) salad.
- Peel and chop turnip and add it with onions, pumpkin and sweet potato to a frittata.

Did you know?

Studies have shown garlic can reduce cholesterol, improve antioxidant levels in the blood and enhance flexibility of blood vessels, although more research is needed.

The humble spud

Potato has a high satiety index. This means they're very filling—a little bit of spud can fill a big hole.

What to do with leftover potato

- Make a potato salad with a canola, sunflower or soybean oil mayonnaise, chopped chives and drained canned four bean mix.
- 'Smash' them and sprinkle with dried rosemary and a drizzle of virgin olive oil (not mashed smooth, just crushed).
- Slice thinly and combine with evaporated skim milk, nutmeg and spring onions, top with a sprinkling of grated parmesan cheese and finish under the grill.

8: Fruit

Enjoying fruit daily can help to control cholesterol and protect your heart. Studies looking at links between diet and disease patterns show people who eat the most fruit and vegetables have the lowest risk of cardiovascular disease. They also have less chance of having risk factors for CVD such as high blood pressure, obesity and type 2 diabetes. How does fruit do it?

There's no clear-cut answer to this one yet; however, the protection probably due to a combination of factors. Substances sharing the limelight are soluble fibre, vitamin C, an array of phytochemicals including carotenoids (such as beta-carotene), folate and potassium. It may also be because fruits are relatively low in kilojoules, satisfying due to their high water and fibre content, and for their gentle effects on blood glucose levels.

Fruit is one of the sweet things in life, and a great example of naturally delicious foods that are both good to eat and good for you. In many cases fruit meets the need for speed and convenience—after all it comes in its own packaging, ideal for eating on the go! Enjoy fruit every day in every way you can. But remember to wash unpeeled whole fruit before eating to remove dirt, bacteria and any farming chemical residues.

No single fruit contains all of the heart-healthy nutrients and phytochemicals. The best advice is to enjoy a variety of different fruits to ensure you're getting a broad spectrum of health benefits, and make the most of what's in season. Some fruits, however, do appear to have 'star' quality, and are worth eating as often as you can. Berry fruits, citrus fruits and apples have emerged as being particularly protective, and are known to be packed with heart-friendly nutrients and phytochemicals.

As with vegetables, the clues to phytochemical and nutrient content are in the colour. In some cases the bright colours are in the skin. So don't peel away the goodness and fibre. Wash the fruit and eat the skin where possible.

Did you know?

Olives, avocados and tomatoes are technically fruits. Olives and avocados are exceptions to the rule that fruits are virtually fat-free—fortunately the fat is mostly the healthy monounsaturated type and good for the heart.

Are you getting enough?

Most health authorities recommend at least two servings of fruit a day. A serving is an average sized piece, such as a medium sized apple, pear or orange, or two smaller pieces, such as plums or kiwi fruit.

What is a serve?

- 1 medium piece of fruit (about 180 g/6½ oz) such as an apple, pear, peach or orange
- 1 cup of fruit pieces such as sliced strawberries or melon
- 2 small pieces of fruits (about 80 g/2¾ oz each) such as plums or apricots
- ⅔ cup (160 ml/5¼ fl oz) of fruit juice

Is fresh best?

Although fresh is usually best, there are lots of great ways to enjoy fruit—canned, juiced, dried, pureed, stewed, baked, frozen—and they all provide valuable nutrients and phytochemicals.

However, there are some vitamin losses with processing. For example, high temperatures involved in cooking, canning and drying fruit reduces the vitamin C and B-vitamin content. As with vegetables, cooking fruit in little or no water is best to prevent leaching of vitamins into the cooking water.

Freezing fruit quickly after picking preserves nutrients well. Juicing can actually increase the availability of phytochemicals because the cells are split open. Drinking fruit juices as close to the time of juicing is a good idea as some losses due occur during storage. Supermarket fruit juices are generally pasteurised (heat treated to make them safe), which causes some vitamin C (ascorbic acid) to be lost, but it is generally added back and is a natural preservative.

Watch what you drink

A freshly squeezed fruit juice is certainly a delicious and nutritious option, however beware of large serving sizes that may contain the juice from 5–6 pieces of fruit and the kilojoules to match. The kilojoules in fruit juice are similar to those in soft drink (soda)! Ask for the smallest size you can.

How to get your 'two fruits a day'
Breakfast

- Blend fruit such as banana, berries or mango with low fat milk and yoghurt for a breakfast smoothie.
- Cut up a selection of stone fruits; peaches, nectarines and plums and top with low fat yoghurt.
- Top wholegrain breakfast cereal with sliced fruit such as strawberries, banana or canned fruits such as peaches, apricots, pears or prunes.
- Enjoy a small serve of fresh juice (top up with cool water for maximum refreshment and less sugars).

Lunch

- Combine sliced apple with reduced fat cheese on a wholemeal bread salad sandwich.
- Segment an orange and serve with a tuna and wholemeal pasta salad.
- Combine dried fruit like raisins, apricots and dates with grated carrot and cottage cheese to fill a multigrain roll or flat bread wrap.

Snack

- Include a piece of fresh fruit in your lunchbox, such as a crisp apple, juicy orange or mandarin, or satisfying banana ready for that snack attack.
- A small handful of dried fruit such as apricots, apple, dates or sultanas/raisins or tropical dried fruits such as paw paw, pineapple and mango with currants.

Dinner

- Add fresh mango slices to a prawn or chicken vermicelli and vegetable salad with chilli and lime dressing.
- Add dried fruit like sultanas to spicy sauces and casseroles such as Moroccan tagine or Indian curry or stir into the rice or couscous to accompany these dishes.
- Add sliced fresh pear to a green salad with walnuts
- Microwave pear pieces with pumpkin, onion and salt-reduced stock and puree. Top with shredded cooked lean chicken, natural yoghurt and coriander for a quick winter soup.

Dessert

- Finish with stewed fruit with low fat custard (use the microwave to save time).
- Bake a fruit crumble.
- Serve a refreshing fruit salad and low fat ice cream.
- Prepare a warm spiced fruit compote.
- A bunch of chilled grapes add a delicious touch of sweetness to complete a meal.
- Try fresh figs served with low fat ricotta and a drizzle of honey.

Quickies for 2

Grilled Banana with Cardamom and Walnuts

A perfect dessert to serve at barbecues.

Make a syrup by heating ½ cup water, 1 teaspoon brown sugar and 1 teaspoon ground cardamom and stir until the sugar has dissolved. Simmer until the sauce has reduced by half. Barbecue or grill 2 bananas, cut in long slices, until browned. Serve each banana drizzled with syrup, a scoop of low fat ice-cream and sprinkled with a tablespoon of walnuts.

Tropical Fruit Salad in Coconut

A great way to enjoy tropical fruits when they are in season—make ahead and chill well.

Combine 1 cup each of drained canned or fresh lychees, mango and pineapple chucks. Mix through torn mint (about 1 tablespoon). Sweeten ¾ cup chilled light coconut milk with ½ teaspoon brown sugar and serve drizzled over the fruit. (Evaporated skim milk and a few drops of coconut essence can be substituted for coconut milk).

Citrus fruit
What are they?

Clementine

Cumquat

Grapefruit

Lemon

Lime

Mandarin

Orange

Pomello

Satsouma

Tangelo

Tangerine

Why they are good for you

Limes were the lifesaver of choice for early explorers to prevent scurvy on long sea voyages and their life-saving continues to this day along with their other citrus fruit cousins. Citrus fruits are very nutritious and rich in vitamins such as vitamins C and B-group (including folate), minerals such as calcium, potassium, phosphorous and magnesium, and fibre. Citrus fruits are also loaded with over 170 different phytochemicals such as carotenoids, flavonoids, coumarins, terpenes, hydroxycinnamic acid, and phytosterols. These phytochemicals have both antioxidant and anti-inflammatory effects.

A typical orange contains 60 mg of vitamin C, which is enough to meet the entire day's Recommended Dietary Intake (RDI). Population studies show high vitamin C intakes are protective against heart disease.

Try adding citrus zest to desserts, juices, stir-fries and cakes and muffins for a real flavour boost. Citrus zest can be removed using a grater or special zester that cuts small curls. Take care not to take too much of the pith as this can be bitter. Citrus peel can also be dried in a sunny spot—keep in a sealed jar after it hardens and add to meat dishes.

A word of warning

Some prescription medications, including heart drugs, interact with natural phytochemicals in grapefruit. Check with your doctor.

How to get more

- Squeeze fresh orange juice for breakfast or try a juiced tangelo.
- Try lime juice with a dash of iced tea on ice for a pre-dinner (non-alcoholic) mocktail.
- Start the day with ½ grapefruit sprinkled with a little sugar.
- Pack an orange, clementine, satsouma or mandarin in the lunch box.
- Use citrus juices and zest for sauces, stir-fries and salad dressings.
- Add orange juice to carrot soup.

- Make a salad with sliced orange, legumes, finely sliced radish, torn fresh basil and lemon juice vinaigrette.
- Add sweetened chopped citrus pulp to cakes, pancakes and muffins.
- Add grapefruit, pomello or orange slices to mixed salad leaves and sliced avocado in a vinaigrette dressing to serve with chicken or seafood.
- Add chopped orange, ginger and fresh coriander to coleslaw.
- Prepare a creamy salad dressing with lemon or lime juice, low fat plain yoghurt and mustard.
- Stir together a quick lemon or lime mayonnaise with juice, zest, chopped dill and prepared mayonnaise (great with heart-healthy seafood).
- Create tempting refreshments by adding sliced lemon, tangerine or lime to cool water.
- Combine slices of pink (ruby) grapefruit, beetroot and Spanish onion with radicchio and vinaigrette dressing for an 'in the pink' salad—complements all hot and cold lean white meats.
- Dollop cumquat marmalade on steamed white fish, chicken or asparagus for a great taste.

To extract the most juice, try microwaving oranges, limes and lemons for around 15 seconds before juicing. Alternatively, roll them under your hand using firm pressure on a flat surface.

Quickies for 2

Orange and Date Couscous

Serve as an accompaniment to Moroccan tagines and Indian curries or add some diced cooked chicken breast, baby spinach and extra orange juice and serve as a salad.

Remove skin, pith and seeds from 1 orange and chop flesh. Bring ¾ cup water and chopped orange to the boil and stir in ¼ cup chopped dried or fresh dates. Remove from the heat. Stir in ¾ cup instant couscous, cover and stand for 2 minutes. Add a teaspoon of polyunsaturated margarine spread, fluff it up with a fork and stir in ¼ cup toasted chopped almonds.

Thai Lime Tofu and Noodle Salad

Chopped Thai basil or Vietnamese mint would be delicious mixed into this salad.

Make a dressing of the juice and zest of 1 lime, 3 teaspoons sesame oil, ½ teaspoon fish sauce, ½ teaspoon each of minced chilli and ginger and 1 teaspoon sugar. Taste and adjust flavours to liking. Toss dressing through 1½ cups cooked rice noodles, ¾ cup fine capsicum strips, ¾ cup sliced green onions and ½ cup fine carrot sticks. Top with 200 g (7 oz) sliced tofu and 1 tablespoon finely chopped roasted peanuts.

Berries
What are they?

Berries are juicy, fleshy fruits that contain one or many seeds. They look gorgeous, taste divine and add beautiful colours as well as nutrients to many dishes. There are many berries, but some of the most popular and readily available are:

Blackberry

Blackcurrant

Blueberry

Boysenberry

Cranberry

Gooseberry

Cape gooseberry (physalis)

Juniper berry

Loganberry

Mulberry

Raspberry

Redcurrant

Strawberry

Youngberry

Did you know?

Botanically, grapes, tomatoes, papaya, pomegranates, durians, lychees and persimmons are berry fruits. Cherries share the rich colours and high phytochemical content of berries, but are actually a stone fruit like apricots and plums.

Why they are good for you

Berries are leaders of the pack when it comes to phytochemical content, being packed full of antioxidants. They contain a variety of phenolic antioxidants (such as ellagic acid and quercitin), which help reduce oxidation of cholesterol in the body. Rich blue-purple colour indicates the presence of anthocyanins and proanthocyanins.

The darker the colour, the higher the anthocyanin content. Anthocyanins actually become more available with juicing. Anthocyanin is used as a natural food colouring. Berries are also rich in vitamin C.

Keep berries in the fridge to retain their nutrient and phytochemical content. Store on some absorbent paper in a single layer to keep them dry and prevent squashing.

Berries are rich in pectin, a type of soluble fibre. Pectin is essential in jam making because it helps the fruit and sugar thicken. This is why berry fruits make good jams and conserves. Look for 'pure fruit' and 'low sugar' jams and preserves for more fruit and less sugar.

How to get more

Berries are delicious and most nutritious eaten raw, but they are highly seasonal so supplement your berry cravings with frozen, dried and canned berries. Phytochemical losses are small after cooking, but heat-sensitive vitamin C content does decline. Luckily this is not a worry as vitamin C levels are high to start with.

- Add a handful of berries to your wholegrain breakfast cereal, such as muesli.
- Blend some fresh, frozen or canned berries, such as blackberry, raspberry or mixed berries, into a smoothie with low fat milk.
- Add some fresh or frozen berries to wholemeal pancake batter and serve with berry conserve and low fat ricotta.
- Sprinkle some fresh or frozen blackberries, raspberries or loganberries onto low fat ice-cream.
- Stir through fresh, canned or frozen berries through some vanilla flavoured low fat yoghurt.
- Mix some berries into fruit crumble: try raspberry/mulberry and apple; strawberry/boysenberry and rhubarb; blueberry/youngberry and pear.
- Add berries to wholemeal (bran) muffins.
- Scatter red berries such as blueberries, strawberries and raspberries over cut watermelon.
- Garnish roasted meats with fresh or frozen redcurrants, blackcurrants or cranberries.
- Add crushed juniper berries to cabbage or mix with wholegrain breadcrumbs, onion, dried currants and herbs for meat stuffings.

Quickies for 2

Berry Trifles

Try a combination of mixed berries in this trifle and use different flavoured jellies for variety.

Layer evenly between two serving glasses: 2 Italian sponge finger biscuits, broken into pieces, 1 cup berries, such as strawberries, raspberries or blueberries, ½ cup chopped raspberry jelly and 1 cup low fat pouring custard. Top each with a few shavings of dark chocolate and serve with another sponge finger on the side.

Berry Spiders

Make delicious fresh or frozen berry 'spiders' for a refreshing snack or quick dessert. Pop the serving glasses in the freezer for a few minutes for extra chill. Pop a ½ cup scoop berries, a scoop of low fat ice-cream and ⅓ cup diet ginger ale into two glasses (pour slowly!).

Berry Sauce

Serve this sauce with lean grilled or barbecued meats. Heat 2 teaspoons extra light olive oil and cook 1 sliced onion, 2–3 minutes. Add 1½ cups fresh or frozen berries and ¼ cup salt-reduced stock and ½ cup freshly squeezed orange juice. Add a dash of port or orange liqueur and simmer, until the berries are soft and the sauce has reduced. Stir while cooking.

- Enjoy the versatility of gooseberries by tossing through salads or making quick desserts.
- Chomp on fresh strawberries or cape gooseberries for a low-kilojoule snack any time.

Apples

What are they?

There's some truth behind the saying, 'an apple a day keeps the doctor away'! Apples are one of the most popular fruits and they're also a 'star' fruit for helping to lower cholesterol and keep the heart healthy. Red, green or somewhere in between, eat apples for enjoyment and for their many health benefits.

Why they are good for you

Apples are rich in soluble fibre, vitamin C and phytochemicals. They also contain potassium and vitamins K and B6. Apples are one of the richest sources of flavonoids (a group of antioxidants) in typical Western diets. The special combination of phytochemicals in apples has been shown to reduce the oxidation of cholesterol, the process that contributes to 'hardening of the arteries'.

There are more than 6000 named varieties of apple! The phytochemical composition of apples can vary, so eat different kinds to ensure you get your full quota of protection.

Apples are known as a 'pome' fruit along with pears, nashi and quince. Apples and other pome fruits have a low GI (glycemic index), which means their natural sugars have a gentle effect on blood glucose levels, and their energy is longer lasting. Low GI foods play a helpful role in reducing the risk of diabetes and cardiovascular disease. Apples also have relatively low energy density, or kilojoules (calories) per gram. In effect they fill you up without being 'fattening'.

What is soluble fibre?

Fruits such as apples are rich in soluble fibres, such as pectins and gums. As well as helping to keep the bowel healthy and slow down the absorption of sugars into the bloodstream, soluble fibres have the ability to reduce blood cholesterol levels. It is thought at least 10 g per day (and up to 25 g), is required for cholesterol lowering.

Soluble fibre content of fruit

1 small orange	1.8 g
4 apricots	1.8 g
½ small mango	1.7 g
1½ dried figs	0.4 g
1 small pear	1.1 g
1¾ cups strawberries	1.1 g
1 small apple	1.0 g

From: Li et al. Journal of Food Composition and Analysis 2002;15:715-723

In a study of 5133 healthy middle aged adults in Finland followed up over 20 years, those who ate the most apples had a 43% lower risk (women) or 19% lower risk (men) of dying from heart disease compared to those who ate the least amount of apples.

How to get more

Fresh is best to maximise nutrients and phytochemicals; however, variety is the spice of life and apples are delicious baked, dried, canned and juiced. Heating does reduce nutrient content, so cook for as little time as possible, and without water so as to reduce leaching of the water-soluble vitamins such as vitamin C. Eating apples with the skin means you will obtain more vitamin C, flavonoids and antioxidants. Apple juice usually has the goodness of the fibre removed, so eat whole apples more than juice.

- Add chopped apple to porridge with a little cinnamon and honey.
- Soak grated apple and apple juice with rolled oats and nutmeg overnight for Bircher muesli.
- Top hot fruit toast with unsaturated margarine spread, cinnamon, sugar and sliced fresh apple.
- Serve stewed or canned apple on wholewheat or buckwheat pancakes.
- Add quartered green apple to a platter with low fat ricotta dip, oven-baked pita chips, dates and dried apricots.
- Snack on fresh or dried apple and almonds.

- Serve apple sauce with lean roast pork.
- Saute sliced apple with cabbage as a side dish— serve with hot and cold white meats.
- Make a fruit frappe by blending together whole apple with skin, ice, lemon juice, mint and ginger.
- Add chopped apple to curries, such as beef, lamb, vegetable or chickpea curry.

Apples go brown due to enzyme activity. You can reduce browning by brushing the cut surface with lemon juice, and reducing exposure to the air by slicing as close to the time of eating as possible. To keep your apples fresh and crisp for longer, store them in your refrigerator in the crisper section or in a plastic bag on the shelf.

TIPS FOR APPLES

Apples and spices such as cinnamon, cloves and nutmeg make perfect partners. Their acidity also combines naturally with low fat yogurt, ice-cream, ricotta or fromage frais, and is balanced nicely with a little sugar or honey. The more tart tasting (sour) apples go beautifully with reduced fat cheese.

Quickies for 2

Spiced Apple Compote

Try this compote on its own or with a dollop of low fat yoghurt, custard or ricotta cheese or serve it on cereal. Make up a cup of tea with a tea bag. Gently simmer eight wedges of an apple in the tea with a cinnamon quill (broken into three pieces), and three cloves until tender. Sweeten to taste with honey. Remove cinnamon and cloves before serving.

Apple and Prune Crumble

Crumbles are always popular, try this topping with other fruit bases. Combine 1 cup cooked apple, 1 tablespoon finely chopped prunes, and grated zest of ½ lemon. Spoon into individual serving dishes and top with ½ cup toasted muesli mixed with ¼ cup well drained low fat ricotta cheese and 2 teaspoons brown sugar. Grill until golden about 1–2 minutes.

Apple and Pistachio Salad

A great side salad with a tomato and cos salad for grills, barbecues and cold meats. Fabulous in a crusty grain bread roll with lean beef and tomato.

Combine 1 chopped green apple (skin on) with ½ cup sliced celery, 1½ tablespoons chopped pistachios and 1½ tablespoons canola and soy bean oil mayonnaise.

9: Herbs and spices

Herbs and spices add flavour and enjoyment to food in lots of interesting and exotic ways. Herbs are the fresh edible leaves and stalks of culinary plants, while spices are the fruit, seeds, buds, flowers, roots or bark and are usually in a dried form. Cooking with spices is a central feature of cuisines from around the globe and lucky for us, a myriad of herbs and spices are readily available for us to experiment with.

Why they are good for you

Herbs and spices make healthy eating a joy. They add fantastic flavour without the use of excessive fat or salt. A grilled chicken breast is not very exciting on it's own, but dry-marinated in smoked paprika, pepper, chilli and garlic takes your taste-buds away on a wonderful journey! Being plant foods, they also contain an array of natural phytochemicals.

Can they lower cholesterol?

Herbs and spices have been used as food and for medicinal purposes for centuries. Traditionally, using herbs and spices in cooking was thought to protect from disease. Although modern research is in its infancy, results so far indicate some fact behind the folklore. Herbs and spices that have been shown in animal and human studies to lower cholesterol or reduce cholesterol oxidation include turmeric, chilli, garlic, fenugreek, cumin, curry leaf and mustard seed. Phytochemicals such as curcumin, capsaicin, and essential oils are thought to be the active ingredients. Herbs and spices also have other heart-friendly effects such as lowering blood sugar levels and triglycerides, increasing the flexibility of blood vessels and reducing oxidation of cholesterol.

The research evidence just isn't strong enough to recommend certain spices over others, but they all add interest, variety and great taste so eat them for pure enjoyment and let your imagination run wild!

A word of warning

Eating herbs and spices in food is safe; however, taking herbs in tablet form carries some risk. Just because herbal supplements are natural doesn't mean they are harmless. For example, garlic tablets can reduce the ability of your blood to clot and can cause bleeding. Talk to your doctor before taking any supplements.

How do we eat them?

- Toast fruit bread and top with honey, low fat ricotta and cinnamon for a delicious breakfast.
- Add a dash of powdered nutmeg and cardamom to skim milk, a banana and a spoonful of wheat-germ for a spicy smoothie.
- Add a couple of bay leaves and paprika, or bouquet garni, to a vegetable soup and serve with a warmed multigrain roll.
- Add tagine spice mix or Ras el hanout to meat/legume and vegetable casseroles to transform them into exotic Moroccan inspired delights—serve with couscous or rice.
- Mix lots of chopped curly or flat leaf parsley through vegetable soups, stews and casseroles or sprinkle over any pasta or rice dish.
- For bread with a Middle Eastern flavour, brush lite wholemeal pita bread with canola or olive oil and sprinkle with Za'atar before warming under the grill. Serve as an accompaniment to chick pea and vegetable tagine.
- Add a vanilla bean to skim milk when making a custard and serve with stewed peaches.

- Use fresh or dried herbs such as oregano, marjarom, parsley and basil to make pasta sauces more authentic. Serve with wholemeal pasta and a crisp green lettuce and fresh basil leaf salad.
- Toss torn Vietnamese mint leaves, Thai basil leaves, finely shredded kaffir lime leaves and finely sliced chilli through hot and cold noodle dishes.
- Make a rich and hearty chilli con carne (lean mince and kidney beans) with Mexican chilli powder. Serve with steamed brown rice and a green salad.
- Dry marinate strips of lean chicken or pork in star anise or Chinese five spice before stir frying with fresh garlic and ginger and combining with vegetables—serve with steamed (brown) rice or (soba) noodles.
- Make a delicious spiced dip by pureeing cooked or canned lentils and powdered cumin, pepper, coriander and caraway—serve with carrot and capsicum sticks, wholemeal pita bread crisps or microwaved pappadums.
- Stir-fry par-cooked potato cubes in a non-stick pan with a little canola oil and panch phora for a North Indian twist to the humble spud. Also great served cold as a salad with low fat yoghurt and crushed garlic dressing.

Spice it up

A grilled chicken breast, lamb cutlet, steak or fish fillet is not very exciting on its own, but dry-marinating before cooking can transform it into something wonderful and take your tastebuds on a culinary journey.

Ian 'Herbie' Hemphill from Herbie's Spices in Rozelle created the following chart showing it is possible to use the same nine ground spices in varying proportions to create a spice blend to create the flavours from five different cuisines. To quote Ian: 'Each quantity can be teaspoon, tablespoon, mug or bucket!' but we suggest teaspoons for household quantities.

Make up the blends, label them and store out of direct sunlight to have on hand whenever a specific cuisine takes your fancy. Use your blend to dry-marinate chicken, beef, lamb or fish and then add the 'plus' ingredient for the complete flavour sensation.

TIPS FOR HERBS AND SPICES

- Dried herbs and spices will lose flavour over time. Buy in smaller quantities.
- Fresh herbs have a milder flavour that is very fragile. Add these at the last minute to hot dishes and just heat through in order to keep their flavour and colour. Fresh herbs are perfect served in salads.
- Prepared curry pastes are mixtures of herbs and spices mixed with a little oil. They are a great way to transform basic meat and vegetable ingredients into authentic Indian and Thai dishes.
- Fry the curry pastes in a little canola or peanut oil to release maximum flavour.

Ground Spice	Moroccan	Middle Eastern	Chinese	Indian	Mexican
Coriander seed	8	4	3	5	2
Cumin seed	4	2	1	8	5
Cinnamon quills	3	8	3	4	3
Turmeric	5	½	¼	3	½
Pepper, black	½	2	1	2	1
Chilli, dried	½	2	1	3	2+
Paprika, mild	2	12	¼	1	10
Cloves	¼	3	2	1½	¼
Star anise	¼	¼	4	1	¼
'Plus'					
Fresh ingredient	Lemon	Mint	Reduced-salt soy	Tomatoes	Coriander leaf

Quickies for 2

These quickies are all made using the spice blends made up from 'Herbies' spice chart. They are great for a salt replacement.

Lamb and Pumpkin Tagine

Enjoy the tastes of Morocco—this tagine could also be made with lean chicken or beef. Adding the lemon zest and juice to the couscous is a great way of incorporating the 'plus' fresh ingredient into the dish.

Heat 1 tablespoon olive oil and brown 200 g (7 oz) cubed lean lamb leg chops, 3–4 minutes. Add 1 tablespoon of Moroccan spice blend, 1 teaspoon each of crushed garlic and ginger, a sliced medium onion and cook, stirring for about 1 minute.

Add 2 cups diced pumpkin (1-cm/½-inch cubes) and water to just cover the meat. Cover and bring to the boil. Reduce heat and cook until the lamb is tender and the pumpkin is cooked, about 20 minutes. (If the sauce is too juicy, cook uncovered for a few minutes to reduce the liquid.) Stir in a teaspoon honey. Serve over couscous tossed in lemon zest and juice to taste with green beans and sprinkle with lots of chopped parsley and two teaspoons toasted slivered almonds.

Spicy Chinese Pork Noodles

For even spicier noodles serve some sliced fresh chillies on the side—a great way to achieve the desired heat level.

Cook 90 g (3 oz) soba noodles according to the packet directions. Drain. Heat 3 teaspoons peanut oil and brown 100 g (3½ oz) lean pork strips, 2–3 minutes. Add ¾–1 tablespoon Chinese spice blend and stir for a few seconds. Add ½ cup sliced spring onions (shallots), 1 cup finely sliced carrot, a bunch of sliced Chinese broccoli (250 g/9 oz) and about ½–1 cup water and stir-fry for 2–3 minutes or until the pork is cooked. Add the noodles and stir until hot. Stir in 1 teaspoon each of salt-reduced soy sauce and sesame oil.

Pureed Lentil and Vegetable Soup

For some crunch, add canned drained chickpeas or white beans after the soup has been pureed and before reheating. Heat a tablespoon sunflower oil in a saucepan and add a tablespoon Indian spice blend and stir for a few seconds. Add ½ cup chopped onion and stir until the onion is coated. Add ½ cup chopped parsnip, 1 cup diced pumpkin, ½ cup red lentils and about 2½ cups of water to cover the vegetables and lentils. Cover and bring to the boil. Reduce heat and cook, stirring occasionally, for about 30 minutes or until the lentils are tender. Puree the soup, reheat and stir through ½ cup diced fresh tomatoes and serve topped with low fat plain yoghurt and sprinkled with lots of chopped coriander or parsley. Serve with warmed lite wholemeal pita bread.

Beef and Bean Corn Bread Parcels

Corn flat bread (or lavash or wraps) are a perfect way to wrap up the Mexican spiced beef and beans into a neat parcel, and is also lower in sodium than many other breads.

Heat 3 teaspoons canola oil and cook, stirring, 1 tablespoon Mexican spice mix and ½ cup sliced onion for 1–2 minutes. Add 200 g (7 oz) lean mince and brown, 2–3 minutes. Add ½ cup drained canned kidney beans and 1–2 tablespoons water and cook, stirring occasionally, for about 3–5 minutes or until the mince is cooked. Spoon mixture into the centre of two flat breads and fold up like parcels. Serve with a salad of 1 cup diced tomato, ½ cup each of corn kernels and diced green capsicum tossed in a tablespoon smooth low fat ricotta and a couple of tablespoons of chopped coriander.

Middle Eastern Chicken and Vegetable Skewers

Use this idea for beef or lamb and vegetable skewers or try rubbing the spice blend on trimmed lamb cutlets. Cube 200 g (7 oz) chicken breast fillet and rub it in 1–2 tablespoons of the Middle Eastern spice blend and marinate for 30 minutes. Thread the chicken onto skewers that have been soaked in water for 30 minutes, alternating with cubed capsicum, mushrooms and zucchini and barbecue or grill until cooked as liked. Serve with a barbecued eggplant, tomato and chickpea salad and with a tablespoon of low fat plain yoghurt mixed with chopped mint.

10: Wholegrains

There's no question about it. Wholegrain foods deserve star billing when it comes to good nutrition for the heart. Eating these foods made from the entire grain (the starchy endosperm, fibrous bran and the vitamin-rich germ) regularly is associated with reduced risk of many chronic diseases, including heart disease, stroke, type 2 diabetes and some cancers. How do they do it?

Wholegrain foods contain more fibre, vitamins, minerals, essential unsaturated fats, trace elements and phytochemicals such as antioxidants, phytoestrogens and plant sterols than their processed counterparts because many of the protective components in grains are contained in the outer layers that are lost in the milling process. Many wholegrain foods also have a low GI (glycemic index), which means they are slowly digested. This not only helps you control your blood glucose and insulin levels, but plays a useful role in your diet if you need to lose weight as these foods will keep you feeling fuller for longer.

Eating a diet rich in wholegrains can reduce your risk of heart disease. In a study of 27 000 men aged 40–75 followed for 14 years, those who ate the most wholegrains had a 20% lower risk of heart disease.

From the traditional to the trendy, carb-rich wholegrains are bursting with energy providing us with protein, dietary fibre, vitamins and minerals. A staple in many parts of the world, they are ideal as the basis for satisfying meals and snacks for everybody. They also play a part with weight control. Did you know that people who eat more wholegrain foods tend to maintain a healthy weight?

Wholegrain foods are made from cereal grains such as wheat, corn, oats, rye, rice and barley with the endosperm, germ and bran layer present in the same proportion as the original grain. For example mixed grain bread or wholemeal bread

Are you getting enough?

Australia's National Heart Foundation says there is a significant association between wholegrain intake and lower risk of cardiovascular disease. They recommend at least 6 g of fibre from wholegrains daily. This is equivalent to 3–4 slices of wholegrain bread, or a serve of wholegrain cereal and 2 slices of wholegrain bread. The USA food guide called MyPyramid encourages Americans to eat half all their grain food servings as wholegrains.

What is a serve?

2 regular slices wholegrain bread
1 thick slice wholegrain bread
1 wholemeal crumpet
1 wholegrain English muffin
1 small pita pocket bread
1 wholemeal thin flat bread/mountain bread/lavash
1 small wholegrain bread roll
4 rye crispbreads
4 wholegrain wheat crispbreads
3 brown rice cakes (thick)
6 rice/corn thins
2 wholewheat breakfast biscuits

1 cup wholewheat flake-style cereal

½ cup muesli

⅔ cup cooked oats (⅓ cup dry)

1 muesli bar

1 cup cooked wholemeal pasta or spaghetti (40 g/1½ oz raw)

1 cup cooked buckwheat noodles

½ cup cooked brown rice (2 heaped tablespoons /40 g/1½ oz raw)

½ cup cooked, bulgar/burghul Grano, Kamut®

⅔ cup amaranth, quinoa

⅔ cup cooked barley, buckwheat, millet, Teff

⅔ cup cooked, Freekeh™ (2 heaped tablespoons dry)

1 cob corn (corn or maize is a grain although often classified as a vegetable)

* Uncooked/dry wholegrains swell to 2–3 times their size with cooking. Check the pack to calculate how much to prepare to equal the servings above

What wholegrain is that?

Check out our star billing grains to look for on the shelves of your supermarket, health or organic food store.

Amaranth is a gluten-free, protein-rich grain whose protein is of high quality. Use it to make porridges, add it to soups, stews and stuffings or to grain-based salads.

Barley is rich in soluble fibre—great for lowering cholesterol and slowing down the release of energy (glucose) into the blood after eating it. Pearl barley is used in cooking to make lemon barley water, pilafs and stuffings or add to soups, stews, salads and desserts.

Buckwheat is related to rhubarb and has a high level of rutin, an antioxidant that can lower blood fats and reduce LDL cholesterol oxidation. You can buy the whole buckwheat grains themselves, toasted groats or buckwheat flour for cooking. Or enjoy products made with buckwheat flour like soba noodles.

Bulgar/burghul is precooked and dried wheat grains. It's quick cooking and convenient to use in side dishes, pilafs or salads such as tabbouleh.

Emmer (farro/grano farro) is an ancient strain of wheat that's making a comeback as a specialty food such as semolina flour made from emmer used for pasta.

Freekeh™ is roasted green wheat, harvested young and thus rich in nutrients. It is high in fibre and has a low glycemic index (GI). Can be served as a side dish, added to soups, salads and burgers, or the flour can be used to make breads, loaves and muffins.

Kamut® is another heirloom grain making a come-back. Kamut grain can be used making hot and cold breakfast cereals, muesli, bread, biscuits and pancakes or served as a side dish.

Maize (corn) isn't officially a vegetable at all, it's a grain. Cooking corn actually increases the levels of antioxidants. Enjoy it on the cob, adding kernels to soups and stews, popping corn or any way you wish.

Millet is often used to make porridge or flat breads or mixed with other grains or toasted before cooking.

Oats contain a type of soluble fibre called beta-glucan that has cholesterol-lowering effects. They are a favourite for breakfast cereals from porridge to mueslis (granola) and muesli bars.

Quinoa isn't a true grain. It is related botanically to Swiss chard and beets. It cooks in about 10–12 minutes, making it ideal as a carb accompaniment for a main meal or for a breakfast porridge. You can also add it to soups and salads and to your baking.

Rice Brown rice retains the bran that surrounds the kernel so it is slower to tenderise and cook than white rice, but it is chewier and nuttier, more valuable nutritionally. White rice has had the bran and germ removed and is more tender to the bite and delicate in flavour.

Rye is unusual among grains for the high level of fiber in its endosperm—not just in its bran. Because of this, rye products generally have a lower glycemic index.

Sorghum also called milo, is a gluten-free grain.

Spelt (old wheat variety) can be used in place of common wheat in most recipes.

Teff is the smallest cereal grain in the world. Today it is getting more attention for its sweet, molasses-like flavour and its versatility; it can be cooked as porridge, added to baked goods, or even made into 'teff polenta'.

Triticale is a hybrid of durum wheat and rye and can be used as a substitute for wheat flour in baking.

Wheat Make the most of wheat in many different forms. Bulgar and grano make excellent side dishes. Wheat berries (whole wheat kernels) can also be cooked as a side dish or breakfast cereal, but must be boiled for about an hour, preferably after soaking overnight. Cracked wheat cooks faster, as the wheat berries have been split open, allowing water to penetrate more quickly.

Wild rice actually isn't rice but the seed of an unrelated American aquatic grass. It takes longer to cook than white rice and is relatively expensive to buy. It is often sold as a white rice wild rice mix with a shorter cooking time because it has been precooked and dried.

What about bread, pasta and breakfast cereals?

If you like to sit down to toast made from white bread for breakfast, and enjoy steamed white rice with your takeaway, keep in mind that, delicious though they can be, these foods have something missing—they have been refined and some of their nutritional goodness is gone. For example, white bread and flour have no bran or germ and are less nutritious as a result.

However, if you're not enthused by bread with intact grains, you'll be pleased to know that wholemeal bread can still be a wholegrain food—provided it is made from whole grains. Rolling, crushing, cracking and extruding whole grains just changes the texture and wholegrains processed in this way are still good for you. Here are some wholegrain processed foods to look for:

- Breakfast cereals labelled 'wholegrain'
- Wholemeal bread
- Wholemeal pasta
- Crispbreads labelled 'wholegrain'

Sodium alert

Healthy as they are, some packaged wholegrain foods such as breads, crispbreads and even some breakfast cereals are higher in sodium than is ideal for a heart-healthy eating plan. In particular, buy bread with the lowest sodium level you can find. Less than 400 mg per 100 g is good, but lower is better.

What about bran?

Grain foods with bran added are higher in fibre and that's good, but they're not always made with wholegrains and therefore not as healthy as wholegrain foods.

Wholegrains have been found to contain equal amounts, or even higher, of antioxidants than vegetables and fruits. Aim to eat at least half your daily grain foods as wholegrains.

How to get more

- Start your day with wholegrain breakfast cereal with low fat milk, topped with seasonal summer fruits.
- Add interest to porridge with stewed rhubarb or quinces or kiwi fruit and mandarin or dried fruit, nuts, seeds and a little honey.
- Choose wholemeal bread made with whole wheat or whole rye for toast and sandwiches.
- Swap to wholemeal pasta and brown rice or start with half white and half brown.
- Substitute some or all the white flour with wholewheat flour, triticale or sorghum in baking berry muffins, nutty biscuits or cookies and fruit or vegetable breads/loaves and cakes.
- Adapt basic risotto and pilaf recipes by adding brown rice, wild rice, grano or millet.
- Snack on popcorn (skip the salt and sugar) or wholegrain muesli (granola) bars.
- Add wholewheat flour, buckwheat flour, or amaranth to pancake or pikelet batter.
- Experiment with tabouli (cracked wheat) salad by trying other wholegrains such as quinoa, buckwheat or millet. Add herbs like basil, coriander or mint or even try adding a touch of a favourite spice.
- Add millet, freekeh or buckwheat to vegetable and meat curries.
- Prepare a savoury tart base using cooked wholegrains (e.g. teff) pressed into the base of a greased pie dish.

Grain porridge

You can make porridge with any wholegrain. Follow the cooking directions on the pack, or, add one part whole grains (e.g. oats, cracked wheat, spelt, kamut, millet, barley, amaranth, quinoa) to four parts boiling water and a pinch of salt and simmer for around 20 minutes, or until tender. Add sugar, honey or maple syrup and your favourite dried fruits such as raisins or mixed dried fruit. Top with a little low fat milk, yoghurt or soy milk.

Quickies for 2

Linseed, Rice, Oat, Raisin and Apricot Porridge

This recipe makes about one and a half cups of porridge. Bring 1½ cups water to the boil. Stir in 2 tablespoons each of linseed (flax seed), brown rice and traditional rolled oats, cover, reduce heat and simmer for about 25 minutes or until the rice is tender. Stir occasionally to prevent sticking. Stir in 1 tablespoon each of chopped raisins and dried apricots and stir for a couple of minutes until the porridge is thick. Serve with soy or low fat milk.

Wholegrain Ricotta and Banana Toast

Choose bread stacked full of wholegrains like wheat, barley, rye, oats, corn (maize) and seeds like sunflower, sesame, poppy and linseeds, and choose the brand lowest in sodium. Sliced apple would be a delicious substitute for the banana.

Mix together 1 teaspoon brown sugar and 1 teaspoon ground cinnamon (or to taste). Slice a banana, drizzle with a little lime or lemon juice and sprinkle the sugar cinnamon mix over it. Toast two thick slices of bread and top each slice with about a ¼ cup fresh low fat ricotta cheese, the banana and juice.

Oats
What are they?

Oat flour

Oatmeal

Rolled oats

Scottish/Irish oats

Steel cut oats

Whole oats (groats)

Why they are good for you

Oats contain a type of soluble fibre called beta-glucan that has cholesterol-lowering effects. They do this by increasing the excretion of cholesterol out of the body, and reducing cholesterol made by the liver. Eating oats has also been shown to benefit people with diabetes. This is probably due to their low GI.

All oats are good for you; however, oat porridge made the old-fashioned way with whole oats (traditional rolled oats) has a lower glycemic index (GI) than instant or quick oats. This is because quick oats have been milled to a finer texture for faster cooking time.

Quickies for 2

Bircher Muesli

A great start to the day—just like a breakfast take-away from your own fridge as it was prepared ahead and ready to be enjoyed!

Combine ½ cup natural muesli with 2 teaspoons each of LSA mix and wheatgerm. Stir in a grated apple, a pinch of ground cinnamon and about ¼ cup of low fat plain or vanilla yoghurt. Refrigerate overnight and serve with an extra dollop of yoghurt the next morning and perhaps a little milk.

Citrus, Sultana and Oat Cakes

This is a variation on the traditional rock cake recipe; quick to make and quick to bake. Enjoy one or two freshly baked and freeze the rest for later—thaw and warm for that sweet snack attack!

Preheat an oven to moderately hot 200°C (400°F/Gas Mark 6). Mix together 1 cup self-raising wholemeal flour, ¼ cup sugar, 2 tablespoons traditional rolled oats, 1½ tablespoons chopped mixed peel and 1 tablespoon chopped sultanas. Melt 1½ tablespoons salt-reduced unsaturated margarine (or plant sterol-enriched) spread and add it to a beaten egg, 1 tablespoon light milk and ¼ teaspoon vanilla essence. Mix the liquid and dry ingredients together—the mixture should be moist and firm (add a touch more milk if needed). Spoon ten mounds onto a tray lined with baking paper. Bake for about 10 minutes until golden.

How to get more

Try these delicious ideas with oat porridge (oatmeal) for a hearty breakfast:

- Cook with mixed dried fruit.
- Swirl through some warmed poached dried figs, apricots and peaches.
- Cook with sliced banana and a dash of nutmeg.
- Cook with chopped apple and cinnamon.
- Top with plain low fat yoghurt and a drizzle of honey.
- Top with brown sugar or maple syrup.
- Top with a spoon of unsaturated margarine spread for a savoury flavour.
- Try muesli boosted with oven roasted macadamias or hazelnuts for variety at breakfast, or as a topping for low fat yoghurt or ice-cream.
- Choose a wholegrain breakfast cereal with oats.
- Select wholegrain bread with oats for sandwiches.
- Add oats to dried fruit and nut mixes for snacking.
- Try oat flour in orange or berry cup cakes, healthy slices, biscuits, pancakes and cookie recipes.
- Use oats as a filler for meat loaf, meatballs, patties and burgers.

Barley
What is it?

Barley flour
Breads and breakfast cereals made with barley
Hulled barley
Pearled barley
Rolled barley

Why it is good for you

Barley is rich in soluble fibre—great for lowering cholesterol and slowing down the release of energy (glucose) into the body.

How to get more

- Make rolled barley porridge for breakfast. Cook 1 part barley in 3 parts water, and allow around ¾ cup raw barley per person. Cook in large batches and freeze leftovers.
- Combine barley with steamed rice (or on its own) to serve with stir-fries, curries, tagines and other wet sauces
- Add barley to soups and stews, such as minestrone.
- Choose wholegrain breads and crispbreads that contain barley.
- Cook barley ahead and have in the fridge ready to add to salads, such as rice, mixed bean or leafy garden salads.
- Combine rice and barley for a healthy risotto.

Quickies for 2
Tuna and Barley Salad

The barley adds a lovely nutty taste and great texture to this salad.

Mix together 1 cup cooked cold barley, 2 cups mixed salad leaves, a diced medium cucumber (seeds removed) and 2 diced medium tomatoes. Add a 185 g (6½ oz) can drained tuna in springwater chunks, 10 black olives and a dressing of 1 tablespoon canola or soy bean oil mayonnaise mixed with 2 teaspoons of lemon juice and chopped garlic to taste.

Teriyaki Beef and Barley Stir-fry

A tasty recipe to serve with crisp lettuce leaves—eat with or wrap in the lettuce like sang choy bow. A great example of 'extending' meat with wholegrains—great for the body and the budget.

Spray a hot pan with olive oil spray and stir-fry about ¾ cup sliced spring onions (using the green part), and ½ cup sliced red capsicum for about 1–2 minutes, set aside. Spray the pan again with oil and add 160 g (5½ oz) lean minced beef, browning well and stirring until cooked for about 5 minutes. Add 1 cup cooked barley, 3 teaspoons terikayi sauce, the onions and capsicum and stir until hot. Serve sprinkled with ¼ cup diced cucumber and the cos lettuce leaves.

11: Legumes

Eating legumes regularly is one of the components of the Mediterranean diet that is associated with lower risk of heart disease. They are champion foods when it comes to health benefits. They are known to lower cholesterol. They may also help to lower high blood pressure. They're also great for those watching their weight. How do they do it?

Legumes are naturally low in fat and high in protein, fibre, vitamins, minerals and phytochemicals. Their cholesterol lowering ability is due mostly to their soluble fibre content, but also because of the protein and phytochemicals they contain. A low GI makes them satisfying and long lasting foods that are particularly helpful for those with diabetes, or at risk of diabetes.

Legumes are the edible seeds of plants with special nodules on their roots that help them obtain nitrogen. This ability increases the protein content of their fruit (seed) that we enjoy eating.

Dried peas—green split, yellow split, chickpeas, black-eye, soup mix

Dried beans—borlotti, butter, cannelini, haricot, kidney, lima, mung, navy, soy

Lentils—green, brown, red, puy, split lentils (Indian dahls)

The peanut is botanically a legume, but is nutritionally similar to nuts and thus usually grouped with them.

Did you know?

Falafels are made from ground legumes.

Hummus is made from chickpeas.

TVP stands for Texture Vegetable Protein and is made from soy and wheat protein.

Finger on the pulse

You may have heard the term 'pulses and legumes' to describe these foods. The term 'pulse' is used interchangeably with legumes.

The vegetarian advantage

Because legumes are so high in protein and other valuable vitamins and minerals, they have long been enjoyed as a meat alternative. Studies on vegetarians have shown much lower risk of chronic diseases such as heart disease, diabetes and cancer, and enhanced longevity. Their high plant food intake—including legumes—is thought to be a significant protective factor.

Are you getting enough?

The National Heart Foundation (Australia) recommends eating legumes in two meals a week, but this is an absolute minimum because legumes add so many important nutrients to your diet. Aim to include them as often as you can.

What is a serve?

½ cup cooked beans or peas or lentils (canned, drained)

120 g (4¼ oz)tofu (soy bean curd)

80 g (2¾ oz) tempeh (fermented soy bean cake)

1 large bean/vege burger (120 g/4¼ oz)

Home cooked or canned?

All legumes must be cooked to make them digestible. With the exception of lentils, legumes must be soaked for at least 4 hours (preferably overnight) before boiling to reduce the cooking time. You can freeze cooked legumes in meal size batches and defrost as needed.

Canned legumes are a nutritious and quick alternative—just drain, rinse and use. Canned legumes contain more sodium than home-cooked legumes prepared with no added salt.

How can you enjoy more legumes?

Legumes have a mild, slightly nutty taste and will take on the flavour of whatever you add them to. Their chewy texture adds interest and their protein and fibre content give a dish filling power.

Breakfast

- Baked beans on wholegrain toast.
- Fill an omelette with a mixture of red lentils, tomatoes, mushrooms and green onions.

Lunch

- Combine canned, drained three or four bean mix, cherry tomatoes, finely chopped onion and parsley with a vinaigrette dressing for delicious bean salad.
- Include brown lentils or soup mix (a combination of legumes) to soups and casseroles.
- Add cannellini beans to a tuna salad.
- Add mung bean sprouts to sandwiches, salads and stir-fries.
- Make warming winter soups with vegetables such as carrot, celery, onion, parsnip, split peas, water and a little salt-reduced stock and serve with oven-baked wholemeal rolls, topped with a little reduced-fat cheese.

Dinner

- Substitute half the mince for cooked red lentils for a Bolognese pasta sauce.
- Combine soaked or canned lentils with mince for meat loaf and serve sliced on wholemeal buns, topped with a chopped tomato, onion and green capsicum salsa and with lots of salad for an open burger.
- Add butter beans to a low salt, tomato-based pasta sauce for a wholemeal vegetable lasagna.
- Cook puy (French green) lentils in salt-reduced vegetable stock until tender and serve as a side dish for lean steak or chicken with sweet potato wedges and salad.
- Add red kidney beans to chilli minced beef for chilli con carne and serve with mashed avocado and a lettuce, capsicum and red onion salad.
- Substitute meat or chicken with chickpeas or beans in curries and casseroles.
- Cook brown rice with red lentils for two-colour rice and serve with spicy Indian dishes.
- Cook and lightly mash brown lentils with chopped herbs—try served under cooked chicken breast or fish with a salad.
- Add borlotti or kidney beans to a potato salad and serve with barbecued or grilled fish steaks with green salad.
- Include a serving of dahl with naan bread when dining in or taking out Indian food.
- Top a baked potato with chilli beans and serve with a green salad.

Snacks

- Dip into hummus with carrot or celery sticks.
- Enjoy a bean-topped bruschetta.
- Nibble on a few roasted chick peas (available in packets and in bulk from nut-sellers).
- Microwave a few pappadums on a sheet of absorbent paper—they are made with lentil flour—and enjoy them alone or with a low fat yoghurt dip such as tsatsiki.

Wind warning

If you're not used to eating legumes, introduce them gradually to avoid problems with wind (gas) caused by the presence of indigestible sugars (oligosaccharides). Discard the water they have been soaked or canned in. Wind becomes less of a problem over time as the digestive system gets used to legumes. Sprouted legumes (e.g. mung bean sprouts) contain less oligosaccharides and are less 'windy'.

Quickies for 2

Hummus

This recipe makes 8 serves, so store leftovers in the refrigerator. Blend together 1 can (425 g/15 oz) drained and rinsed chickpeas, ⅓ cup tahini (sesame) paste, the juice of 2 large lemons, 2 tablespoons extra virgin olive oil, and 2 cloves fresh garlic, until smooth.

Hummus, Carrot and Baby Spinach Wrap

Spread 2 wholemeal flat bread (lavash) with 2 tablespoons light plant sterol spread and ½ cup hummus. Divide 1 cup grated carrot and 1 cup of baby spinach leaves between the wraps and roll each up tightly.

Chilli Bean Melt

Choose either a chilli sauce to suit your taste, the filling would be great in taco shells with salad. Could also be made on salt-reduced wholemeal bread.

Cut the tops of 2 wholegrain crusty bread rolls and scoop out the bread from the centre (make bread crumbs out of the scooped out bread and tops and freeze to use later). Spread the inside of the rolls with 2 tablespoons light plant sterol spread. Mix together ½ cup each of diced green capsicum, 1 medium fresh tomato, 2 teaspoons hot chilli sauce and 1 cup drained and rinsed four bean mix. Spoon the bean mixture into the rolls and top each with 2 teaspoons grated low fat, salt reduced cheese. Grill until warmed through and the cheese melts. Serve sprinkled with chopped parsley.

Soy foods

What are they?

Breads and breakfast cereals containing soy such as soy and linseed breads

Miso (fermented soybean paste)

Soy cheese

Soy custard

Soy grits

Soy milk

Soy pasta

Soy yoghurt

Soybeans

Tempeh (fermented soybeans)

Tofu (soybean curd)

TVP (textured vegetable protein)

Vegetarian meat alternative products such as burgers, patties and sausages

Why they are good for you

Soybeans are the highest in protein of all legumes, and the protein is of the highest quality—similar to animal protein. Soybeans are also high in fibre, vitamins, minerals such as calcium, zinc and iron, and trace elements. Diets high in soy protein have been shown to lower cholesterol, reduce cholesterol oxidation, reduce triglycerides and blood pressure, increase good HDL cholesterol and help keep blood vessels more flexible.

Although low in fat, the type of fat in soy is the healthy polyunsaturated type—including some omega-3. Soybeans are also rich in bioactive peptides and isoflavones—a type of phytochemical. Isoflavones are also called phytoestrogens (plant oestrogens) and have a number of health benefits including reduced risk of hormone-related cancers (e.g. breast and prostate). The phytochemicals in soy have also been found to have antioxidant and anti-inflammatory effects.

A diet with a combination of heart-friendly foods (soy protein, plant sterols, nuts and foods rich in soluble fibre like oats, barley and psyllium) has been shown to equal the effects of statin drugs in people with high cholesterol.

How much soy protein?

The optimal amount of soy protein for cholesterol appears to be around 25 g a day, but every little bit counts—especially when combined with other cholesterol-lowering dietary components in a diet low in saturated fat. It is also good to eat soy foods several times a day rather than all at once for best effects. Uncooked soy foods such as milk, yoghurt, tofu and tempeh may be better than baked goods such as protein bars and muffins because the bioactive peptides stay intact.

Is it OK for men to eat phytoestrogens?

The answer is yes; soy foods are good for everyone. Women and men in Asian societies have consumed soy foods for thousands of years. In fact, these societies have much lower risk of chronic diseases and soy foods have been identified as an important part of their protective diet.

Soy protein content of soy foods	
½ cup soy flour	18 g
Tempeh (100 g/3½ oz)	18 g
Soy beans (boiled, 100 g/3½ oz)	15g
Tofu (100 g/3½ oz)	15g
Soy beans (canned, 100 g/3½ oz)	10 g
1 cup (250ml/9 fl oz) soy milk	8.8 g
Soy burger (60 g/2¼ oz)	7.8 g
2 slices soy & linseed bread	7.7 g
1 tub soy yoghurt (200 g/7 oz)	6.6 g
TVP vege-mince, prepared (125 g/4½ oz)	5.3 g
45 g/1½ oz soy breakfast cereal	5 g

Note: These are approximate and may vary. Check food labels

How to get more

- Tofu and tempeh are ready to eat and don't require cooking; however, they are delicious fried in healthy oil until golden brown, or just heated through in soups and stir-fries.
- Choose breads and breakfast cereals that contain soy (e.g. soy-linseed bread) for toast and sandwiches.
- Make your own breakfast cereal using soy flakes, traditional rolled oats, dried fruits and nuts.
- Try soy milk on your breakfast cereal.
- Vary sandwich fillings with tempeh or soy cheese as a protein option.
- Enjoy soy yoghurt as a healthy snack with a swirl of pureed fruit or berries.
- Add tofu or tempeh to your Asian vegetable stir-fries .
- Sprinkle diced tofu or tempeh over soups or salads.
- Substitute soy-containing flour (e.g. gluten-free flour) for wheatflour in baking.
- Include a vegetarian meat alternative such as soy burgers, soy patties or soy sausages.
- Make a soy smoothie with soy milk and fresh fruit.
- Add drained and rinsed canned soybeans to salads, soups and stews.
- Grill marinated (hard) tofu and vegetable kebabs on the barbecue.
- Use miso to create soups, stocks, marinades.
- Substitute normal pasta with soy pasta.
- Use TVP instead of mince in pasta sauce, 'meat' loaf and lasagna.
- Serve hot fruit puddings or seasonal fruit with soy custard for dessert.

Quickies for 2

Marinated Tofu and Vegetable Kebabs

Great for the barbecue. Serve with rice salad or a green salad and fresh wholegrain bread. Marinate 200–250 g (7–9 oz) of hard tofu cubes of in salt-reduced soy sauce and sweet chilli sauce. Thread onto skewers along with slices of capsicum (pepper), zucchini (courgette) and mushroom and barbecue or grill lightly on all sides.

Sesame Tofu and Vegetable Noodles

This noodle dish can also be served chilled as a salad.

Heat 1 tablespoon canola oil and stir-fry 200 g (7 oz) cubed hard tofu until golden, set aside. Add 2 cups frozen stir-fry vegetables and stir-fry for about 2–3 minutes. Add 1½ tablespoons hoi sin sauce and about a tablespoon water and stir-fry for a minute. Stir in 1 cup fresh hokkien noodles and tofu and stir until hot. Serve sprinkled with a tablespoon toasted sesame seeds.

TVP Bolognese

Prepare TVP as per packet directions to make 200 g (7 oz) of TVP mince. Heat 1 tablespoon olive oil and cook 1 chopped onion and 1 teaspoon crushed garlic until soft, about 2–3 minutes. Add the drained TVP and 1½ cups no added salt canned crushed tomatoes, 1 tablespoon of no added salt tomato paste, 1 teaspoon of Italian herbs, cover and simmer for 10–15 minutes, stir occasionally. Toss in 1 cup cooked wholemeal pasta, heat and serve with a fresh garden salad.

Soy-Good Breakfast

This provides around 10 g (½ oz) of soy protein per serve. Divide 2 cups of a commercial soy-based break-fast cereal between two bowls. Pour around 200 ml (7 fl oz) of soy milk over each and top with 100 g/3½ oz (½ tub) of soy yoghurt and ½ cup chopped fresh fruit.

TOFU TIP

Ensure you choose the right tofu for the dish. You need 'hard' or 'firm' tofu that can be sliced to add to stir-fries and soups. Silken tofu is best to blend/puree for desserts or dressings.

What is nut meat?

Nuts and seeds are important foods for vegetarians because of the protein and minerals like iron and zinc they provide. 'Nut meats' are a combination of diced nuts and seeds held together in a loaf with herbs and spices that can be sliced and enjoyed as a meat alternative—available in supermarkets.

NUTS AND SEEDS TIP

Because of their unsaturated (healthy) fat content, nuts and seeds must be stored correctly to prevent them going stale (rancid). Store nuts and seeds in an airtight container away from light and heat, and eat soon after purchase. To keep them longer, store in the fridge or freezer.

Almonds
What are they?

Almond meal

Blanched almonds

Flaked almonds

Raw almonds

Roasted almonds

Slivered almonds

Why they are good for you

Almonds are high in protein, calcium, vitamin E and arginine (a heart-protective amino acid). They also contain good amounts of fibre, iron and zinc. A study looking at the effects of adding almonds to the usual diet found they contributed significant amounts of monounsaturated (healthy) fats, fibre, vitamin E, magnesium and copper—all positive nutrients for heart health. Eating more almonds also had the effect of reducing undesirable nutrients—trans (bad) fats, sodium, cholesterol and sugars.

In a statistical analysis of the best dietary combination to reduce the risk of heart disease, almonds were included along with wine, fish, dark chocolate, fruits, vegetables and garlic. Researchers concluded this combination of foods consumed regularly could reduce cardiovascular disease events by 76 per cent, could increase life expectancy of men by 6.6 years, and 4.8 years for women.

How to get more

Raw or roasted almonds, and (puréed) almond butter are just as good for you and will equally help get your cholesterol down—even salted almonds have benefit, but unsalted are best in order to limit sodium which may increase blood pressure.

- Add slivered or chopped almonds to muesli.
- Top fruit and yoghurt with slivered almonds.
- Enjoy almond butter on wholegrain or fruit toast.
- Snack on raw almonds with skin.
- Substitute some flour with almond meal in baking.
- Add roasted almonds to a chicken and vegetable stir-fry.
- Toss slivered almonds through steamed or microwaved carrots or broccoli.

Quickies for 2

Red Cabbage, Almond and Orange Salad

This is a fresh crunchy side salad that's high in fibre. Add a cup of chopped barbecued chicken with the skin removed and a wholegrain roll for a light meal, or enjoy on its own as a super-healthy snack (also delicious in a flat bread wrap with cottage cheese). Great with Middle Eastern chicken and vegetable skewers (see page 65).

Mix together 2 cups finely shredded red cabbage, ½ cup grated carrot, ¼ cup sliced celery and chopped chunks of a peeled orange (pith and seeds removed). Spray a non-stick pan with oil and lightly brown ¼ cup slivered almonds, cool and sprinkle over the salad to serve.

Rocket and Almond Pesto

A peppery version of a traditional basil pesto. Serve a dollop on grilled fish, chicken or soup or toss through pasta.

Place 2 cups baby rocket leaves, 1 tablespoon slivered almonds, 1 teaspoon each of crushed garlic and grated parmesan cheese and 2 teaspoons olive oil in a small blender or food processor and blend until combined. Makes about ⅓ cup (4 tablespoons).

- Combine raw almonds with dried apricots for a tasty snack.
- Add chopped roasted almonds to rice, noodle and couscous dishes.
- Stir whole raw almonds into a four bean mix, herb, tomato and asparagus salad.
- Toast flaked almonds and sprinkle on baked fish.
- Add almond meal to meat loaf, meat balls, burger patties and fish cakes.
- Coat lean meat such as pork or chicken in crushed almonds and bake.
- Top fruit puddings and parfaits with roasted slivered almonds.
- Bake apples or pears with a filling of chopped almonds and mixed dried fruit.
- Top healthy fruit cakes with blanched almonds for a decorative finish.

Walnuts
What are they?

Raw walnuts

Walnut halves

Walnut pieces

Roasted walnuts

Why they are good for you

Walnuts are the highest in polyunsaturated (healthy) fats—including omega-6 and omega-3 type—of all nuts. They are rich in fibre and protein, and also contain vitamin E, folate, manganese (a trace element) and arginine (an amino acid), tannins and polyphenols (phytochemicals).

Omega-3
Thirty grams (1 oz) of walnuts (approx. 20 walnut halves) contains around 2 g of plant omega-3 fat (alpha linolenic acid)—meeting the suggested daily amount for adults.

Eating walnuts can lower your cholesterol.
An Australian study of people with type 2 diabetes compared the effects of low fat diets with and without walnuts. The cholesterol level of the subjects who just followed a low fat diet did not change, whereas the subjects who ate walnuts reduced their LDL (bad) cholesterol by 10% and increased their HDL (good) cholesterol by 30%.

How to get more

- Top oat porridge with sliced banana, nutmeg and chopped walnuts.
- Sprinkle chopped walnuts over stewed apple and cinnamon.
- Present a platter of whole walnuts in their shell after dinner.
- Enjoy walnut halves with raisins or dates as a snack.
- Add walnuts along with dried fruit to scones, cakes and biscuits (cookies).
- Add chopped walnuts and sultanas or raisins to coleslaw.
- Create a wonderful pasta dish by adding steamed vegetables, chopped walnuts, olive oil, cracked black pepper and the juice and zest of a lemon to hot wholemeal pasta.
- Combine salad greens, walnuts, fresh sliced pear and thinly sliced goats cheese and serve on the side with lean chicken or beef.
- Add walnuts to couscous seasoned with salt-reduced stock, lemon juice, capers and green olives—great served with fish.
- Scatter roasted walnuts on a plate of cut vegetables and dips.
- Crush walnut pieces and sprinkle on the top of smoothies.

Quickies

Pumpkin, Bean, Sage and Walnut Penne

Enjoy this penne hot or cold with a green salad.

Microwave 2 cups diced butternut pumpkin until cooked and mix into 2 cups hot cooked wholemeal penne with ½ cup drained and rinsed, canned kidney beans. Mix together 1 tablespoon olive oil, 1 teaspoon crushed garlic and 1 tablespoon torn sage and stir through the hot penne. Divide between two bowls and top each with 2 teaspoons low fat plain yoghurt and two teaspoons chopped walnuts. Serves 2.

Sweet Spiced Walnuts

Kilojoule (calorie) alert! These are much healthier than lollies, but go easy. This recipe makes 6 servings and is perfect for special occasions—be sure to share! Store in an airtight container in a cool, dark place.

Beat an egg white with 1 tablespoon water. Add 1½ cups walnut halves and mix to coat, draining off any excess egg. Line a tray with baking paper and mix 1 teaspoon each of ground cinnamon and icing sugar together. Sieve a coating of the cinnamon mix on the baking paper and arrange a single layer of walnuts on the top. Sieve the remaining cinnamon mix on top and bake in a moderate oven 180°C (350°F/Gas Mark 4) until the coating has set and the nuts are warm (about 10–15 minutes. Keep a watchful eye on them!). Allow to cool and store in an airtight container. Serves 6.

Linseeds
What are they?

Linseeds (also known as flax seeds)
LSA mix (contains linseeds, sunflower seeds and almond meal)
Breads, breakfast cereals and crispbreads with linseeds

What about flaxseed oil?

There have been very few clinical studies on the effects of flaxseed oil on cholesterol and heart health. Flaxseed oil is highly unstable and thus unsuitable for cooking. It goes 'off' quickly and must be kept in the refrigerator. Go for whole or ground flaxseeds (linseeds) instead.

Soy and linseed: a great combination

Foods containing soy protein and linseeds are good for you. A small study found daily consumption of soy- and linseed-containing foods over 3 weeks resulted in a 10% decrease in total cholesterol and a 12.5% decrease in LDL (bad) cholesterol.

Why they are good for you

Linseeds are rich in three protective nutrients for the heart: omega-3 polyunsaturated fat called alpha-linolenic acid; lignans—a type of phytoestrogen phyto-chemical; and soluble fibre that helps to lower cholesterol.

How to get more

- Add linseeds or LSA mix to breakfast cereals.
- Cook linseeds with oats for porridge.
- Buy breakfast cereals, breads and crispbreads with linseeds.
- Add linseed meal or LSA mix to fruit smoothies.
- Add ground linseeds towards the end of cooking pasta sauce, soups or stews.
- Add ground linseeds to meatloaf or meatballs.
- Add whole linseeds to muffins and biscuits (cookies).
- Toast linseeds and add to rice dishes to have with stews, curries and casseroles.
- Add linseeds to homemade bread.

Whole or ground?

Because linseeds have a tough outer shell, the nutrients are more accessible to the body from ground or crushed linseeds. Chewing whole linseeds well has a similar effect—the inner nutrients are released once the shell is broken.

The omega-3 story

Alpha-linolenic acid is one of the two essential fats required by human beings to stay healthy. Alpha-linolenic acid is plant type omega-3 polyunsaturated fat that is strongly linked to reduced risk of death from heart attack. The richest sources of alpha-linolenic acid are linseeds, walnuts, green leafy vegetables and canola oil and margarine.

Quickies for 2

LSA Thickshake

This shake is satisfyingly rich and sweet with plenty of long lasting energy—great for afternoons or breakfast on the run. You could use skim milk instead of soy.

Place 1 tablespoon of ground LSA mix, 400 ml (13½ fl oz) soy milk, 2 teaspoons malted chocolate drink powder, 2 dried or fresh figs and 2 scoops of low fat ice cream into a blender and blend for 1–2 minutes.

Tomato, Basil, Linseed and Yoghurt Bruschetta

Vary this recipe by adding canned tuna or shaved cooked chicken.

Heat a griddle pan on high heat. Spray two thick slices wholegrain sourdough bread with oil and cook on each side. Rub each piece with a cut clove of garlic. Cut 2 tomatoes and divide between the toasted bread, sprinkle over freshly ground black pepper. Sprinkle each piece with about a tablespoon of torn basil, 1 teaspoon linseeds and drizzle with 1 tablespoon low fat plain yoghurt.

13: Fish

Fish and seafood offer a bounty of nutritional goodness. There is clear evidence that eating fish and seafood regularly protects the heart. In addition, scientists have found that people who eat a lot of fish can have lower rates of depression. How does fish do it?

Fish is rich in protein, a good source of heart-friendly omega-3 fats, contains vitamins A and D, and provides helpful minerals and trace elements such as magnesium, zinc, iron, fluorine and selenium. Fish and shellfish harvested from salt water are the best source of dietary iodine—an essential trace element important for thyroid function and metabolism.

Eating fish is one of the pillars of the healthful Mediterranean diet.

How much fish?

The National Heart Foundation of Australia recommends enjoying at least two fish meals a week, as does the American Heart Association (and they suggest oily fish).

What is a serve?

1 fish fillet 120 g/4¼ oz cooked

Tuna or salmon, canned 85 g/3 oz drained

Sardines, kippers canned 75 g/2½ oz drained

Oysters, 12 large/18 small

Prawn/shrimp, 15 medium

Heart health associations around the world agree that eating fish regularly—fresh, frozen or canned—is a good idea to keep your heart healthy.

All fresh fish and seafood is good for you (unless it's coated in batter and deep-fried).

Make the most of the convenience of frozen fish products if it suits your busy lifestyle, but keep an eye out for saturated fat and sodium (salt) content. Battered and crumbed fish fillets, fish fingers, and fish in creamy sauces may be high—check the label and choose products with the lowest levels.

Canned fish (e.g. tuna, salmon, mackerel, herring, sardines, oysters, mussels) are nutritious options. Opt for fish canned in springwater rather than brine to avoid too much salt. Tuna flavoured with herbs, garlic, onion etc is a tasty option—they can be a little higher in sodium, but you're better off having the fish than not. Sardines in tomato sauce are another enjoyable option if you don't like them plain.

What about cholesterol in shellfish?

While shellfish such as prawns contain dietary cholesterol, they are not significant contributors to blood cholesterol levels. The biggest influencer of blood cholesterol is saturated fat in the diet, and shellfish are low in total and saturated fat. Besides, most people don't consume shellfish often or in large amounts.

Are you getting enough?

People living in Western countries generally fall short of eating the recommended amounts of fish and omega-3 fats for optimum health. Scientific research shows that eating some fish is better than having none.

TIPS WITH FISH

- 1–2 serves a day from the meat and alternatives group is recommended for good health. Select a variety of choices each day, including fish and seafood, to get your 1–2 serves. For a light meal, a half serve is suitable, whereas one serve is good for a main meal.
- When buying fresh fish fillets, aim for 150 g (5½ oz) raw weight per person.
- Anchovies are high in salt; use them sparingly in cooking.
- Compare labels of canned products in sauce to find the lowest in sodium.

Care with mercury

Fish is a heart-healthy food and can be enjoyed regularly as part of a balanced diet, however some groups of people need to take extra care with some types of fish. Some species contain levels of mercury that may be harmful to children and pregnant women if eaten to excess. It is the larger, longer living, predatory fish at the top of the ocean food chain that tend to concentrate mercury in their flesh. Examples include shark (flake), billfish (swordfish /broadbill and marlin), and orange roughy (sea perch)—these should be limited to one serve a fortnight or less by pregnant women and children. Advice on how to limit mercury can vary around the world according to local species and conditions, so check with your local food safety authority.

Cooking fish

People often say the reason they don't eat more fish is they don't know how to cook it. Your fishmonger will be a great help—just tell them what you want to make and they'll suggest a suitable type of fish.

How to get your 'two serves a week'
Breakfast

- Enjoy smoked salmon or trout with a poached egg for breakfast—try a side of steamed spinach and wholegrain toast.
- Arrange canned herring or kippers on a soy-linseed muffin spread with plant sterol spread, and top with fresh rocket (aragula) leaves and a poached egg.
- Brunch on sardines atop wholegrain toast—with cherry tomatoes on the side.

Lunch

- Combine smoked salmon or trout with avocado and salad greens on wholegrain sandwiches.
- Fill sandwiches with tuna or salmon—with coloured lettuce or rocket (aragula), tomato and cucumber.
- Top a cos lettuce, corn and beetroot salad with flavoured canned tuna and a wholegrain roll.
- Enjoy some sushi with salmon, tuna or prawn filling.
- Combine cooked prawns with canola or soy mayonnaise and dill for sandwich filling—along with sliced celery and alfalfa sprouts.
- Mash canned mackerel with lemon zest, chopped chives and a little low fat plain yoghurt for a wholemeal pocket bread or wrap filler.

- Make a fish and lentil soup—cook boneless white fish in simmering, no-added-salt, canned tomatoes, canned lentils, salt-reduced stock and water—stir in lots of freshly chopped parsley just before serving.
- Herrings in tomato sauce make a good topper for toasted grain muffins.

Dinner

- Barbecue or pan fry fish steaks or cutlets—serve with stir-fried rice noodles with snow peas, capsicums and green onions or crisp green salad and wholegrain roll.
- Bake a whole fish stuffed with herbs, onion and lemon wedges—serve with roast potatoes and steamed broccoli and yellow squash.
- Bake fish fillets in foil with fresh coriander, canola oil and lemon or lime slices –serve with a cumin and carrot couscous and steamed green beans.
- Make a fish and pumpkin yellow curry with bone-less cubed fish fillets—serve with steamed brown rice and wilted Chinese greens such as gai lan, choy sum or pak choy.
- Stir-fry baby octopus with garlic and sweet chilli sauce—stir through wholemeal pasta or soba noodles and serve with a watercress, mint and snow pea sprout salad on the side.
- Cook marinara mix (mixed chopped seafood; mussels, prawns, fish, squid), in lots of garlic and canned diced no added salt tomatoes and toss through cooked penne pasta—serve with an endive, fennel and olive side salad.

- Brush fresh tuna or salmon and long slices of yellow and green zucchinis with oil and grill or cook on a griddle pan—serve the tuna topped with the zucchini, baby rocket and drizzled with a citrus dressing.
- Add clams to a brown rice risotto or pilaf—serve with steamed green beans, carrots and cauliflower or a leafy red and green salad of radicchio and mustard greens.

Snacks

- Snack on small cans of tuna or salmon—with wholegrain toast or crispbread.
- Dip prawns (shrimp) into natural low fat yoghurt combined with canola mayonnaise, lemon zest and chopped dill.
- Offer a platter of freshly shucked oysters with fresh squeezed lemon or lime juice and fresh ground black pepper.
- Snack on smoked oysters or mussels on brown rice crackers.
- Enjoy an antipasto plate with marinated baby octopus.
- Start a meal with a selection of sashimi served with salt-reduced soy sauce, pickled ginger and wasabi (horseradish mustard).

The magic of omega-3 fats

Omega-3 fats reduce the risk of having a heart attack (primary prevention), but also reduce the risk of having another heart attack in people who have already had one (secondary prevention).

The two omega-3 fats in fish are called DHA and EPA (docosahexanoic acid and eicosapentanoic acid). Their protection is not from lowering cholesterol, but through a variety of other important effects: they keep the heart beating regularly (prevent arrhythmias), lower blood triglyceride (diacylglycerol) levels, 'thin' the blood and prevent clots, help to calm inflammation, lower blood pressure and keep the walls of blood vessels (endothelium) flexible.

Omega-3 fats are highest in oily fish such as salmon, tuna, mackerel, sardines and herring, however, other fish and seafood provide useful amounts of omega-3 too. There is also a plant type of omega-3 fat called alpha linolenic acid (ALA) found in canola oil, linseeds, nuts and green leafy vegetables and it's also good for the heart (see page 109).

How much omega-3?

Aim for around 500 mg a day of omega-3 fats (EPA and DHA) can significantly reduce the risk of cardiovascular disease. You can get this amount from around half a serve of fish (60 g/2 oz) from the 'excellent' list below. More omega-3 fats (around 1000 mg a day) may be required to prevent a second heart attack if you've already had one—the American Heart Association suggests one serve of oily fish daily (from the 'excellent' below) or a fish oil supplement. Talk to your doctor before taking supplements.

Omega-3 polyunsaturated fat content of Australian fresh and canned seafood (per 100 g/3½ oz))				
Excellent (more than 900 mg)		Great (250–900 mg)	Good (Less than 250 mg)	
Fresh	Canned	Fresh	Fresh	Canned
Swordfish	Red/pink salmon	Sand flathead	Barracouta	Canned tuna
Silver perch	Sardines	Southern sea garfish	Barramundi	
Mackerel	Mackerel	Gemfish	Black Bream	
Queensland mullet	Herring	Blue grenadier	Blue groper	
Blue mackerel	Pilchards	Blue eye	Chinaman leather-	
Sea mullet	Kippers (herring)	Red gurnard	jacket	
Atlantic salmon	Smoked oysters	Jackass morwong	Golden bream	
Smoked salmon	Smoked mussels	Red mullet	John Dory	
Yellowtail scad		Nannygai	Ling	
Tailor		Golden perch	Rock & tiger flathead	
Tarwhine		Australian salmon	Tiger Flathead	
Trevally		Scallop (bay)	Greenback flounder	
Southern bluefin		Snapper	Garfish	
tuna		Spiky oreo	Perch gernard	
		Rainbow trout	Pike	
		King George whiting	Scaber leatherjacket	
		Sand whiting	Orange roughy	
		Oyster	School whiting	
		Pilchard	Tiger prawn	
		School shark	Baby octopus	
		Spanish mackerel	Rock lobster	
		Silver warehou	King prawn	
		Blue swimmer crab	Yabby	
		Squid, calamari	Mud crab	
		Blue mussel		

★ Content is for 100 g raw weight, unless canned.

*Omega-3 fat content can vary between brands of canned seafood, and can vary within the same species of fresh seafood depending on the season and harvest location and conditions.

Quickies for 2

Salmon and Butter Bean Salad with Wholemeal Bread

Mix 2 cups mixed salad leaves with 1 cup sliced capsicum (pepper), 1 cup snowpeas and 1 cup drained and rinsed canned butter beans. Top with 90 g (3 oz) drained canned salmon in springwater (with bones) and a squeeze of lemon juice. Serve with 4 slices wholemeal bread (look for the lowest in salt) spread with 2 tablespoons light plant sterol spread.

Mixed Grain Lemon and Dill Salmon Salad Sandwiches

Make a dressing with the juice and zest of 1 lemon and 1 tablespoon each of chopped dill and parsley. Mix together 1 cup each of baby spinach and baby rocket, ½ cup each of finely sliced red onion and cucumber; stir in the dressing. Spread 4 slices mixed grain bread with barley with 2 tablespoons light plant sterol spread. Evenly divide 90 g (3 oz) drained salmon in springwater and the spinach and rocket salad between two slices of bread and top each with a slice of cold baked kumara (orange sweet potato) and the other slice of bread.

Sardine, Chickpea, Kumara, Spinach and Orange Salad

Combine 3 cups baby spinach leaves, 1 cup of cubed cooked kumara, 1 cup of drained, rinsed canned chickpeas, 1 cup sliced red capsicum and the chopped flesh and juice of 2 oranges. Toss through 150 g (5½ oz) drained sardines in springwater) and serve with 4 slices wholemeal bread with 1½ tablespoons plant sterol enriched spread.

Fish Fill-all (makes 2 main meal serves or 4 light meal serves)

This is great for filling baked potatoes, pita pockets, wraps, sandwiches and rolls. Combine a 210 g (7½ oz) can drained salmon in springwater (with bones), ¼ cup sweet corn kernels, 1 tablespoon finely diced Spanish (purple) onion, 2 teaspoons finely chopped dill or about ½ teaspoon dried dill, freshly ground black pepper and a blend of 1 tablespoon each of mayonnaise (choose brand lowest in sodium) and low fat plain yoghurt.

Fish Fill-all Barley Flat Bread Wrap

This wrap is sure to become a lunch time favourite. Spread 2 pieces of barley flat bread or lavash with a half quantity of Fish Fill-all, 2 cups dark salad leaves and ½ cup mung bean sprouts.

14: Eggs

Don't be surprised to see eggs as heart-friendly foods. While they don't have the protective effects of foods like fish, nuts, legumes and wholegrains, they are a highly nutritious and versatile food that can be included in cholesterol lowering eating plans. How do they do it?

Eggs contain perfect protein—just the right balance of amino acids the body needs. As well as containing cholesterol, egg yolk contains mostly unsaturated fats and 10 vitamins and 8 minerals, including good amounts of riboflavin, vitamin B12 and phosphorus. Egg yolks also contain antioxidants lutein and zeaxanthin. Egg whites are protein and have no fat or cholesterol.

A group of nutrition experts in Australia (Egg Nutrition Advisory Group, ENAG) concluded for those with high cholesterol ' 3–4 eggs per week in the context of a diet low in saturated fat and containing known cardio-protective foods is not associated with increased risk'.

In population studies, eating eggs is not associated with higher cholesterol levels, and research does not support the idea that egg consumption is a risk factor for coronary disease. Heart health organisations around the world no longer say eggs should be avoided, and focus more on having a balanced heart-healthy diet overall.

You can eat whole eggs, omega-3 enriched eggs and egg yolks if you have high cholesterol, but moderation is key. While opinions vary about how many eggs are OK, they don't need to be avoided altogether.

The eggs and cholesterol story

Individual differences in the blood cholesterol response to eating eggs have been found. It is estimated around one third of the population over-react to eating more eggs and will experience an increase in cholesterol (hyper-responders). If you already have high cholesterol, your chances are higher of being a hyper-responder, but don't despair. Just limit eggs to no more than three a week and include plenty of heart-friendly foods. There are also egg-replacer products (frozen or dried) that contain no cholesterol available in supermarkets. Talk to your doctor about monitoring your blood cholesterol levels with any change to your usual eating habits. Cross your fingers and hope you are in the lucky group for whom enjoying eggs makes no difference!

Cholesterol in eggs

Large 60 g egg—225 mg

Medium 55 g egg—200 mg

Small 50 g egg—190 mg

* People with high cholesterol are advised to limit dietary cholesterol to 200mg per day

Eggs and plant sterol spreads—a helpful partnership

If you eat whole eggs that contain cholesterol, it makes sense to use plant sterol spreads daily. Plant sterols are naturally occurring substances that reduce cholesterol absorption from the intestines (see page 110).

Omega-3 enriched eggs

These eggs are produced by providing hens with linseed (flaxseed) enriched feed—naturally rich in alpha-linolenic acid (omega-3 fat). Studies on the effects of high omega-3 eggs have shown positive effects on blood fats—higher HDL (good) cholesterol and lower triglyceride (triacylglycerol) levels. Omega-3 enriched eggs are one of the few foods that contain long chain omega-3 DHA and EPA normally obtained from fish, and so are great for those who can't eat fish.

How to enjoy eggs in moderation
Breakfast

- Serve a boiled egg with wholegrain toast and plant sterol spread (margarine).
- Combine a whole egg with an extra egg white for a light omelette and serve with wholegrain toast with plant sterol spread and grilled tomatoes.
- Top some wholegrain toast and plant sterol spread with a slice of smoked salmon and a poached egg and garnish with fresh dill.
- Scramble an egg with evaporated skim milk and chopped parsely and serve on top of wholegrain rye toast with plant sterol spread.

Lunch

- Pack a boiled egg for a workday lunch and enjoy with vegetable sticks, wholemeal pita bread and a dollop of canola mayonnaise.
- Swirl a lightly beaten egg into homemade simmering chicken and corn soup just before serving for a Chinese style soup.
- Combine mashed boiled egg, low fat cottage cheese and curry powder and use as a filling for wholemeal bread or flat bread wraps with watercress and black pepper.
- Fill a wholegrain roll (spread with plant sterol spread) with a sliced boiled egg, a thin slice of lean ham, wholegrain mustard and baby spinach leaves.

Dinner

- Combine sautéed onions, garlic, dill, mixed steamed vegetables, beaten eggs and low fat ricotta and bake in a non-stick oven dish. Slice and serve with a tossed green salad and wholegrain bread.
- Make a thin plain omelette, cut into long thin strips and add to vegetable and noodle stir-fries.
- Add quartered boiled egg to a main meal salad of mixed greens, cherry tomatoes, cucumber, roasted capsicum, butter beans and tuna canned in springwater. Drizzle with olive oil vinaigrette and serve with crusty wholegrain bread with plant sterol spread.

Quickies for 2

Egg, Rocket, Beetroot and Hazelnut Salad

Enjoy this salad as a light meal with a crusty grain roll or wholemeal bread (check the label to find the lowest in sodium).

Boil 2 small eggs for 7 minutes, cool. Place 2 cups baby rocket leaves, about 8 canned, drained baby beetroots (quartered or halved depending on size) and 2 tablespoons halved roasted hazelnuts in a bowl. Mix 2 teaspoons extra light olive oil, ½ teaspoon each of balsamic vinegar, Dijon mustard and honey until smooth and toss through the rocket. Shell the eggs and quarter and fold through the salad.

Vegetable Frittata

Great for a weekend breakfast to share.

Heat 2 teaspoons canola oil in a small non-stick pan. Add 1½ cups vegetables, cut into fine sticks or diced, such as, carrot, cucumber (seeds removed), zucchini and celery and cook, stirring occasionally, for about 2–3 minutes. Stir in a teaspoon salt-reduced soy and ½ teaspoon sesame oil. Beat 2 small eggs, add to the pan, swirling the pan to coat the vegetables. Cook until the egg is almost set then grill only just to complete the cooking. Invert the frittata onto a warmed plate. Serve topped with baby herbs or leaves.

- Stir-fry mixed Asian-style vegetables and cooked brown rice in a little peanut oil. Fry an egg in a non-stick pan sprayed with oil and serve on top of the vegetables. Garnish with chopped spring onions.
- Boil wholemeal pasta and drain. Stir through sliced boiled egg, pesto, steamed broccoli and asparagus.
- Simmer sliced green beans, capsicum and zucchini strips in fresh tomato puree (or no-added-salt canned diced tomatoes) with canned, drained lentils. Crack one egg per person into the mixture and cook until set. Serve with a scoop of mashed potato and a green salad.

15: Meat, poultry and game

Good news! There's no need to give up eating meat or chicken just because your cholesterol is high. As long as you keep it lean (and that means trimming off all visible fat and removing the skin from poultry) and cook it appropriately, meats can be a nutritious, delicious and satisfying part of a cholesterol-lowering eating plan. How does meat do it?

Choosing lean meats rather than fatty meats will remove a significant amount of saturated fat from the diet, which helps lower cholesterol levels. Lean meats are an excellent source of protein needed for building and repairing body tissues. They also provide iron for healthy blood and energy, zinc for immunity and vitamin B12 for a healthy nervous system. Lean meats also provide some healthy unsaturated fats, including omega-3 similar to those in fish.

Which meats?

All meats with the fat removed are fine. Buy your meat lean to begin with, or trim any remaining fat. Many supermarkets now sell a range of lean meats (perhaps called 'trim', 'lean' or 'heart-smart'), and some have the Heart Foundation Tick. Meats to eat only occasionally due to their high saturated fat and/or sodium content are deli meats like bacon, ham, salami, cabanossi, mortadella, devon, hamburger mince and sausages. Keep an eye out for lower fat versions of ham, bacon and sausages, but keep in mind the sodium is still high.

Lean choices include:

Chicken: skinned chicken breast (lowest in fat), chicken thighs skinned and trimmed, takeaway barbecue chicken, skin removed.

Beef: Lean steak, fat-trimmed roasts (e.g. topside roast and silverside roast), lean stir-fry strips, lean beef mince, diced lean beef.

Veal: (naturally lean) steak, stir-fry, cutlet.

Kangaroo: (naturally lean) e.g. steaks, mini-roasts.

Lamb: lean leg steaks, trim lamb strips, diced trim lamb, trim lamb mini-roast, trim lamb butterfly steak, trim lamb eye of loin, Frenched cutlet (bone left), lean lamb mince, fat-trimmed leg roast (easy carve).

Pork: lean leg steaks, loin steaks, scotch fillet.

Turkey: breast, no skin.

Venison (deer): (naturally lean), steaks, chops, roasts, mince (trim all visible fat if present).

TIPS WITH MEAT

Enjoy lean red meat in 3–4 meals per week for the iron and zinc it contains.

Enjoy chicken and white meats such as pork in 3–4 meals per week to leave room for other heart-friendly sources of protein like fish (at least 2 meals) and legumes (at least 2 meals).

Vegetarians need to replace these with other suitable alternatives, such as legumes, nuts and seeds, taking care to ensure they get enough vitamin B12, iron and zinc—fortified foods and supplements may be needed.

Everyone's nutritional needs are different, so the number of recommended serves of meat will vary. Adult women and men need at least one serve a day, with larger men and more active women up to two. Kilojoule-controlled diets can also have two serves of lean meat to boost nutrients and filling power (see page 147 for eating plans).

Red or white meat—which is best?

Variety is a great strategy; enjoy them all! Check out the following table—you may be surprised how different lean meats compare.

Fat comparison of meats per 100 g (3½ oz) (raw)

Type of meat	Total fat grams	Saturated fat grams	Polyunsaturated grams	Cholesterol mg
Lean lamb	6.2	2.4	0.7	68
Lean beef	3.9	1.6	0.4	57
Veal steak	1.8	0.6	0.4	57
Kangaroo	1.8	0.3	0.3	51
*Chicken breast,	5.5	1.7	0.7	66
*• Turkey breast,	1.6	0.5	0.42	60
Lean pork	4.2	1.6	0.7	59
*• Duck breast	2.5	0.6	0.4	143
Venison	2	0.8	0.4	68
* No skin. Sourced from AUSNUT database and USDA(•)				

What is a serve?

100 g (3½ oz) lean steak, chicken, raw
85 g (3 oz) lean steak, chicken, cooked (½ chicken breast)
½ cup lean mince, cooked (70 g/2½ oz)

How do I cook it?

- Pan fry lean meat in a non-stick pan on low heat with a little spray oil to prevent sticking and serve with rice, noodles or pasta dishes.
- To ensure tenderness, cuts such as beef blade, skirt or chuck, or lamb forequarter chops are best cooked in liquid over a longer time, such as casseroles, tagines, curries and stews.
- Make soups with meats such as chuck, shin, round, brisket of beef or diced lamb forequarter.

How can I enjoy lean meats?

A healthy meal with meat is one that is balanced with plenty of vegetables or salad and some legumes or wholegrains like wholemeal pasta, brown rice, multigrain bread or corn.

Lunches

- Fill a wholemeal roll (low salt) with lean roast beef, mustard, canola mayonnaise, rocket (aragula) and thickly sliced tomato.
- Turkey breast with reduced-fat cream cheese, cranberry sauce, watercress and roast zucchini makes a perfect topping for whole-rye bread.
- Roll up chopped chicken breast and sliced mango with canola mayonnaise, celery slices and mesclun leaves in a lite flat corn bread wrap.
- Make a lean beef pattie and top with salt-reduced tomato ketchup, lettuce, tomato, grated carrot and pineapple on a wholegrain muffin for a great burger.
- Try an open mixed grain bread sandwich with sliced avocado, mignonette lettuce, pastrami and red currant jelly.
- Mix some cooked lean lamb though tabouli and serve in a small wholemeal lite pita pocket with sliced cucumber and a dollop of reduced-fat yoghurt.

Dinners

- Serve roasted lean beef with a fresh chilli and tomato salsa, roasted sweet potato, roasted beetroot and steamed broccoli.
- Enjoy chilli con carne with lean mince, kidney bean and corn salsa on brown rice, accompanied by a green salad.
- Stir-fry lean pork and vegetables with hokkien noodles in plum sauce and toss through some roasted cashews or peanuts.
- Barbecue lean kangaroo or beef, red and green capsicum skewers, eggplant slices and potatoes in their jackets.
- Roast lean turkey breast filled with herbed wholegrain bread stuffing and enjoy with salt-reduced gravy, sweet corn and green peas.
- Char-grill chicken, zucchinis, mushrooms and red capsicum and serve with a side salad of lettuce, corn kernels and tomato.
- Pan-fry veal steak, onion and tomato, mash some potatoes with crushed garlic and accompany with microwaved carrots and green beans.

Meat and weight loss

Protein-rich foods like lean meats satisfy the appetite, and help us feel full. Research has shown that low fat, kilojoule-controlled diets with slightly larger serves of lean meat (and smaller serves of starchy foods like bread and potatoes) have helped people successfully lose weight without going hungry, and are nutritionally balanced.. See page 147 for eating plans.

Quickies for 2

Mediterranean Barbecue Marinade

This is great for red meats such as beef, lamb or kangaroo. Use this amount for 200 g (7 oz) raw meat.

Combine 1 tablespoon extra virgin olive oil, 1 teaspoon crushed garlic, 2 teaspoons lemon juice, 2 teaspoons finely chopped parsley and fresh ground black pepper. Pour over trimmed meat in a sealed container, preferably overnight. Pan fry or barbecue meat, discarding the marinade, and serve with an Italian style salad of mixed lettuce and marinated grilled vegetables in a little balsamic vinegar and chopped herbs.

Grilled Beef, Lamb, Pork or Chicken Open Turkish

This is a delightful variation to a traditional burger. Choose the lowest sodium brand Turkish bread.

Cut 100 g (3½ oz) meat or chicken into two thin slices. Heat a little oil in a non-stick pan and cook meat as liked. Wrap in foil to rest. Cut a slice of wholemeal Turkish bread (approximately 10-cm/4-inch square) through the centre and toast in the same pan. Top each toast with the cooked meat, ½ cup rocket leaves, 3 slices of tomato, 2 slices beetroot and about 2 teaspoons of the condiment of your choice.

Meat with Herb and Garlic Vegetable Pasta

This is the recipe for dinner suggested in the example daily menu for cholesterol lowering—moderate in kilojoules (see page 160).

Heat 1 teaspoon canola oil in a non-stick pan and cook 200 g (7 oz) lean meat as liked. Wrap in foil to rest. Cook 80 g (2¾ oz) wholemeal pasta in a large pot of boiling water. Mix 1½ tablespoons plant sterol-enriched spread, 1–2 tablespoons chopped fresh parsley, chives or dill and 1–2 teaspoons crushed garlic. Microwave 1 cup each of carrot sticks, broccoli and cauliflower florets and stir into drained cooked hot pasta with 1 cup of finely shredded red cabbage and the herb and garlic mixture. Serve with the meat.

Chilli and Garlic Beef and Vegetable Stir-fry

This is the recipe for dinner suggested in the example daily menu for cholesterol lowering—low in kilojoules (see page 159).

Stir-fry 300 g lean beef strips, 1–2 teaspoons each of chopped garlic and chilli in 1 tablespoon hot canola oil for 2–3 minutes and set aside. Add ½ cup each sliced carrot, green onion (spring onions) and mushrooms to the pan and stir-fry for 2–3 minutes. Return the beef to the pan and add 1½ cups finely shredded Chinese greens, 1 cup cooked soy beans and cook until hot. Stir in a few drops of sesame oil before serving sprinkled with chopped coriander.

16: Healthy fats and oils

Fat has been given a bad wrap for too long. Instead of cutting out fat to lower cholesterol, more of the right fats are needed to obtain the correct balance. Healthy oils are heart-friendly foods, so go ahead and make the healthy and tasty choice. How do they do it?

Healthy oils help lower cholesterol in several ways. They can replace saturated fats that increase cholesterol (by substitution) and actively reduce blood cholesterol (by direct action).

Polyunsaturated fats are better than monounsaturated fats at lowering LDL cholesterol, but monounsaturated fats are great for replacing saturates and it's good to have both. Healthy oils also add flavour and enjoyment to other heart-healthy foods.

Fat-free diets are not recommended for anyone, including those with high cholesterol. Some fats are essential—just like vitamins.

The 3-step action plan to get your fats right

Cut right back on saturated fats found in butter, fatty meat, cheese, ice-cream, fried take-aways, biscuits, pies and pastry.

Eat at least 1½ tablespoons per day of added healthy fats like vegetable oils and spreads—both polyunsaturated and monounsaturated.

Use 25 g a day of plant sterol-enriched spread daily.

What are healthy oils?

The healthy oils are the unsaturated types and they fall into two main groups—polyunsaturated and monounsaturated. These terms describe the chemical structure of the main kinds of fatty acids present. The terms omega-3 and omega-6 describe the chemical structure of different kinds of polyunsaturated fats.

Remember:

Saturated is bad and unsaturated is good.

Polyunsaturated fats provide essential omega-3 and -6 fatty acids and are needed for optimal cholesterol lowering and heart health.

Enjoy a combination of both poly- and monounsaturated fats.

Food sources of polyunsaturated fats
omega-6

Brazil nuts

Corn oil

Cottonseed

Grape seed oil

Pine nuts

Safflower

Sesame seeds and sesame oil

Soybean oil and spread

Sunflower oil and spread

Walnuts and walnut oil

Foods containing plant type omega-3 polyunsaturated fat

Canola oil

Linseeds and linseed (flaxseed) oil (see page 88)

Mustard seed oil

Omega-3 enriched eggs

Soy bean oil

Walnuts and walnut oil

Wheatgerm and wheatgerm oil

Foods containing marine type long chain omega-3 polyunsaturated fat

Rich sources—oily fish and seafood (see page 95). Smaller amounts in: omega-3 enriched eggs, fortified foods with added long chain omega-3 such as spreads, milk, bread, small goods.

Food sources of monounsaturated fats

Almonds

Avocado

Camellia (tea) oil

Canola oil and spread

Macadamia nuts and macadamia nut oil

Olive oil and spread

Peanuts and peanut oil

Pecan nuts

Pistachio nuts

Rice bran oil

Essential nutrients

All fats are made up of fatty acids. There are two fatty acids that the body cannot make for itself and must obtain from food. These are termed essential fatty acids—linoleic acid (LA) from the omega-6 family and alpha linolenic acid (ALA) from the omega-3 family.

There are some essential vitamins that are only found in foods that contain fat. These are called fat-soluble vitamins—Vitamins A, D, E and K. For example, vegetable oils are one of the richest sources of vitamin E.

Which healthy oils are best?

It's best to enjoy a combination of both polyunsaturated and monounsaturated oils. A polyunsaturated oil-based spread (for example, sunflower) balances well with olive and canola oils used for cooking. Or, a monounsaturated oil-based spread (such as olive or canola) balances well with sunflower oil or soybean oil used for cooking. Spread is a great substitute for butter when baking.

Let your taste guide you to choose the oil that best suits the dish.

Am I getting enough healthy oils?

The National Heart Foundation of Australia suggests eating 1½ tablespoons per day of added healthy fats like oils and spreads for good heart health.

The amount of healthy oils and spread you should eat will depend on your individual needs (see page 147 for eating plans).

What is extra-virgin olive oil?

The term extra-virgin refers to the oil from the first mechanical pressing of the olives and is low in natural acidity and rich in phytochemical antioxidants and flavour. Normal olive oil is usually a mixture of virgin oil and refined oil. 'Cold pressed' is the name used to describe the first pressing of other types of oils.

Plant type omega-3 (ALA) content of different foods per serve (USDA data)

Food and serve amount	ALA content (g)
Linseed (flaxseed) oil, 2 teaspoons	5.8
Walnuts, small handful	3
Mustard seed oil, 2 teaspoons	1½
Canola oil, 2 teaspoons	1
Soybean oil, 2 teaspoons	0.7
Linseeds, 1 teaspoon	0.6

Do I need plant omega-3?

Yes. The plant omega-3, alpha linolenic acid (ALA), is essential and must be provided by the diet. The Adequate Intakes (AIs) for Australia and New Zealand are 1.3 g per day for men, and 0.8 g per day for women; however, it is recommended to consume more than this (around 2 g) to help reduce heart disease risk.

While marine omega-3 are known for the heart-protective properties, it is now thought that ALA from plants also reduces the risk of coronary heart disease and fatal heart attack in both women and men.

To spread or not to spread?

Many people stop using oil spread when they find out they have high cholesterol but this makes no nutritional sense. To lower cholesterol only saturated fats need to come down, whereas the good polyunsaturated and monounsaturated fats need to take a leading role.

Oil spreads are important sources of healthy fats including essential omega-6 and -3 fats and fat-soluble vitamins. Just in case you're still not convinced, a New Zealand study found that a diet including a spread with plant sterols produced lower cholesterol results than a diet lower in fat without spread.

What's the difference between spread and margarine?

Spreads are the term used to describe reduced-fat 'margarine' by Food Standards Australia and New Zealand (FSANZ). The products you buy in a tub to put on your bread and toast are called 'spreads' because they are less than 80 per cent fat. The hard yellow blocks used for baking are called margarine because they contain 80 per cent fat or more. Many people still use the term margarine when they mean spreads.

Butter or margarine?

This question has been well and truly answered by scientific research. Butter increases cholesterol, while unsaturated spreads help to lower cholesterol—especially if they are enriched with plant sterols. The Heart Foundations in Australia and New Zealand both recommend using unsaturated spread instead of butter. The American Heart Association agrees. This advice is also echoed by The Australian National Health & Medical Research Council in the Dietary Guidelines for Australians.

As a spread for bread and for baking, choose (reduced-salt) unsaturated margarine spreads rich in omega-6 and omega-3, made from canola, sunflower, safflower and olive oil rather than butter or hard margarine ...

(Food for Health; Dietary Guidelines for Australian Adults, 2003)

Case study

A population study conducted in Poland found a clear association between an increasing amount of unsaturated margarine spreads and oils in the diet and a reduction in coronary heart disease risk. During the 1990s consumption of polyunsaturated fat increased by 57% as the supply of affordable canola and soy bean oil margarines increased, and butter became more expensive due to a reduction in government subsidies. The death rate from coronary heart disease fell by 40% over the same period.

What are plant sterol-enriched spreads?

Plant sterols are naturally occurring vegetable fats that have been shown to lower cholesterol. They do this by reducing the absorption of cholesterol from the digestive system which results in more cholesterol being passed out of the body.

Plant sterols can be found in vegetable oils, nuts, seeds and wholegrains, but in quite small amounts. Higher levels are found in plant sterol-enriched spread.

Clinical studies of plant sterols have shown that eating 2 g a day can lower total and LDL (bad) cholesterol by around 10 per cent. This amount of plant sterols is present in 25 g (1 rounded tablespoon) of plant sterol-enriched spread. For best results you need to eat plant sterol-enriched spreads daily and keep eating them to ensure your cholesterol stays down.

Plant sterol-enriched spreads are true 'functional foods' for heart health and an easy way to make a significant improvement in blood cholesterol levels. Australia's National Heart Foundation agrees that 2 g a day of plant sterols (found in 25 g spread) can lower cholesterol by 10 per cent and this effect is additional to the effects of cholesterol-lowering drugs.

Because there can be some small reduction in the absorption of carotenoid antioxidants while using plant sterol spreads, have an extra serve of orange/yellow vegetables or fruits to be on the safe side. While some research suggests the reduction in absorption is insignificant, vegetables and fruits are heart-friendly foods so go ahead and eat more!

What about trans fats?

Trans fats are just as bad as saturated fats in raising blood cholesterol levels. Heart health organisations around the world agree they should be minimised in the diet. Trans fats occur naturally in animal and dairy fat; however, they are also produced in the partial hydrogenation, or hardening, of oils during commercial food manufacturing.

Cooking margarine and shortening used by commercial bakers may be high in trans fats, so pies, pastries, cakes and biscuits can contain significant levels. Look for the words 'partially hydrogenated' on food labels to spot trans fats. Unsaturated spreads made from vegetable oils tend to be low in trans fats, with many being virtually trans-free—check the label to ensure you're buying the lowest. Hard cooking margarines (sold in blocks) also tend to be higher in trans fats, so use spreads for cooking instead.

The Tick program is a helping hand

The Heart Foundation Tick is a helping hand—it helps you out when you need it most—at the supermarket. Foods with the Tick on the label meet the Heart Foundation's strict nutrition standards for saturated fat, kilojoules, fibre and salt and products such as margarine spreads must have less than 1% trans fats to qualify. Foods with the Tick must first be independently tested to make sure they meet strict nutrient criteria and ongoing random audits ensure the foods continue to meet the Heart Foundation's standards.'

Saturated fats to avoid

Saturated fats increase cholesterol and also increase the risk of cardiovascular disease. They also worsen insulin resistance—a key feature of the metabolic syndrome. A rule of thumb is that saturated fats are usually of animal origin, such as butter and lard. However, there are always exceptions! For example,

coconut and palm oil despite being of plant origin are highly saturated and best enjoyed occasionally.

When it comes to healthy eating and lowering your cholesterol, it's what we do most days that really counts. Enjoying the occasional treat won't be a cholesterol disaster, but make sure foods high in saturated fat aren't on your daily menu.

Saturated fat content of foods (daily target < 20 g, the lower the better)	
Food + serving size	Saturated fat per serve (g)
Apple pie, individual commercial frozen	7
Bacon, 1 long rasher	6
Butter, 2 teaspoons	5
Chocolate bar, nougat and caramel filling, 60g/2½ oz	8
Chocolate cheesecake, 1 slice	19
Cream-filled choc coated biscuits, 2	6
Croissant, 1 average	13
French fries, takeaway, small	7
Hamburger with cheese, takeaway	9.5
Meat pie, individual	10
Pasta carbonara creamy style (½ cup sauce)	23
Pizza, ¼ family size supreme	7
Rich vanilla ice-cream, 1 cup	8.5
Salami, 2 slices	5
Sausages, 2 thin	14
*Average figures from FSANZ (AUSNUT)	

What about weight?

It is now clear that low fat diets are not the answer to prevent overweight and obesity. It is the amount of kilojoules (calories) eaten, not the proportion of fat in the diet, that is important for weight control. A 6000 kilojoule weight loss diet containing 30 per cent kilojoules from fat is just as effective as a 6000 kilojoule diet with 20 per cent kilojoules from fat. The 30 per cent fat diet is better because very low fat diets don't provide enough essential omega-3 and -6 fats and fat-soluble vitamins.

For cholesterol lowering, very low fat diets aren't the best because they lower good HDL cholesterol (and aren't very much fun either!). You can include 1½ tablespoons of added healthy oils and spreads in a balanced low-kilojoule eating plan for weight loss, or more if you use a fat-reduced spread (see page 147 for eating plans).

How do I enjoy healthy oils?
Breakfast

- Spread plant sterol-enriched spread on hot wholegrain toast or English muffin and top with orange marmalade—enjoy with some fruit salad and a cup of tea.
- Partner a wholemeal fruit muffin, freshly baked using an unsaturated spread, with a skim latte.
- Brush a thick slice of sour dough or soy and linseed bread with rice bran oil and toast on a griddle pan. Top with sliced avocado and a little smoked salmon and a dollop of low fat ricotta.

- Pan-fry mushrooms in a little grapeseed oil, add a dash of sweet smoked paprika and a squeeze of lemon juice. Serve on a wholemeal crumpet.

Lunch

- Spread wholegrain bread with plant sterol-enriched spread and top with salmon and plenty of salad.
- Dress a tomato, rocket and cucumber salad with extra-virgin olive oil and balsamic vinegar and enjoy with crusty wholegrain bread and tuna in springwater.

Did you know?
Healthy oils contain antioxidants

- Seed and nut oils and rice bran oil contain high amounts of Vitamin E—a powerful antioxidant thought to play a protective role against heart disease.
- Virgin olive oil is known for its polyphenolic antioxidants that can reduce oxidation of LDL cholesterol in the body.
- Rice bran oil contains oryzanol and avocado oil contains Beta-Sitosterol—both plant sterols that help to lower cholesterol absorption and reduce LDL cholesterol levels.
- Grapeseed oil contains proanthocyanidins thought to protect the heart.

- Make a tasty sandwich with lean chicken, soybean oil or canola mayonnaise and plenty of coloured lettuce on wholegrain bread.
- Dress a cos lettuce, red cabbage and orange salad with avocado oil and raspberry vinegar and serve with wholemeal pita bread with slices of cold lean roast pork.
- Toss a kidney bean, sprout and onion salad in a dressing of walnut oil and white wine vinegar and enjoy with drained sardines in springwater and multi-grain crispbreads spread with polyunsaturated spread.

Dinner

- Start an Indian curry by sautéing spices in canola or peanut oil.
- Start an Italian tomato sauce by sautéing garlic, onions and capsicum in olive oil.
- Finish an Asian stir-fry or chicken and corn or vegetable, tofu and noodle soup by adding some sesame oil just before serving.
- Melt some plant sterol-enriched spread into mashed or baked potato.
- Dress steamed/microwaved carrots with walnut oil and a little orange juice and zest.
- Sprinkle mustard seed oil and apple cider vinegar on sautéed cabbage and onion.
- Combine canola oil and dried rosemary to coat potato wedges before bakin.g

- As an entrée serve wholemeal Turkish bread pieces for dipping into a small dish of avocado oil and Middle Eastern dukkah.
- Dress steamed/microwaved Asian greens with a mixture of peanut oil and salt-reduced soy sauce.
- Coat a mix of vegetables such as capsicum, zucchini and eggplant in olive oil before roasting.
- Dress cooked vegetables in a mixture of virgin olive oil, lemon juice, chopped parsley and crushed garlic for a great Mediterranean flavour.
- Make a potato and bean salad with cooled boiled potato cubes, drained 4 bean mix and a mixture of soybean oil or canola mayonnaise, natural yoghurt and a dash of curry powder.
- Drizzle corn on the cob with melted plant sterol spread mixed with chopped herbs.

TIPS WITH OILS

- If you're cooking a stir-fry or curry for 2 people, then use 1 tablespoon of oil. For a family of four, use 2 tablespoons. Measure the oil out rather than pour it straight in. Always add oil to an already hot pan as it will spread more easily to prevent sticking.
- Store spreads in the fridge, and oils in a cool dark place.
- It's best to buy oils in smaller quantities and replace them regularly to ensure your oil is fresh.
- When deep-frying, ensure oil is hot to prevent food soaking up too much oil and cook food in small batches. Use oils with a higher smoke point that remain stable at high temperatures such as canola, soy, safflower, sunflower, peanut, corn or olive oil (deep-frying is a higher kilojoule cooking method).
- Virgin olive oil is not the best for deep-frying as it has a lower smoke point than more refined olive oil. It's also more expensive, so save the good stuff for your salads.
- Use a screw-top jar and shake well to make dressings—store any remainder in the fridge.

Quickies for 2

All-purpose Italian Dressing

Place 3 teaspoons of extra-virgin olive oil, 2 teaspoons of balsamic vinegar, ½ clove crushed garlic and ½ teaspoon Italian herbs in a screw-top jar. Shake to combine, taste and adjust flavours to suit.

Moroccan-style Dressing

Perfect to dollop on a couscous vegetable salad or a couscous made with toasted almonds and dates to be served with a lamb tagine.

Place 3 teaspoons of soybean oil, 2 teaspoons apricot nectar, 2 teaspoons low fat natural yoghurt and ¼ teaspoon Moroccan dry spice blend in a screw-top jar. Shake to combine, taste and adjust flavours to suit.

Avocado Delight

Enjoy a little spooned over grilled fish or chicken and the remainder tossed into a mesclun, tomato and corn salad.

Place 3 teaspoons avocado oil, 3 teaspoons lemon juice, a dash of Tabasco or chilli sauce and 2 teaspoons finely chopped dill in a screw-top jar. Shake to combine, taste and adjust flavours to suit.

DAIRY TIPS

• Evaporated skim milk is a great alternative for cream in cooked savoury dishes and sauces.

• Add coconut essence to evaporated skim milk for Asian-style creamy curries.

• Natural yoghurt is a great alternative for sour cream in dips and soups.

• Ricotta cheese is a great alternative to cream for desserts and cakes.

• Use buttermilk instead of regular milk in baking and pancakes.

Quickies for 2

Indian Yoghurt Dip (Raita)

Delicious with vegetable sticks, pappadums, or as a cooling side dish for curries—each serve contains 280 mg of calcium and is virtually fat-free.

Combine 200 g (7 oz) low fat yoghurt, 2 diced Lebanese cucumbers, 1 clove of crushed garlic and a teaspoon of finely chopped mint or to taste.

Reduced-Fat Cheese Sauce

Great for pouring over steamed vegetables, or as the basis for a creamy pasta sauce—each serve contains 435 mg calcium.

Heat 3 teaspoons unsaturated margarine spread in a small non-stick pan. Add 3 teaspoons plain flour and cook for 2 minutes while stirring. Remove from the heat and gradually add 1 cup skim milk (or soy milk) a little at a time, stirring constantly to remove lumps. When all the milk has been added, place back onto a medium heat and stir until thickened. Add ½ cup of grated reduced-fat cheese and a pinch of nutmeg.

Variations: Add 2 tablespoons of finely chopped parsley or dill, or the juice and zest of a lemon (off the heat to prevent curdling).

18: Alcohol and chocolate

Wine and chocolate are foods that many people love and they can fit into a cholesterol- lowering eating plan, but enjoying them in moderation is the key. Being foods derived from plants, wine and chocolate contain natural antioxidants that may actually be beneficial for a healthy heart.

Alcohol

Taking alcohol 'for medicinal purposes' goes back a long way and now there is considerable evidence that drinking alcohol in moderation may be beneficial—especially for heart health.

Population studies show that people who drink a little alcohol regularly seem to have a lower risk of cardiovascular disease (coronary heart disease and stroke) compared to those who don't drink any alcohol at all. This protection particularly applies for those middle-aged or older and those already at risk of developing coronary heart disease. The reason for this protective effect is not clear. It might be due to other protective lifestyle factors like exercise or a healthy diet, or it may be that alcohol enhances the absorption of other protective dietary factors.

What about red wine?

Wine has been of interest to nutrition researchers for years because of the so-called French paradox. This term was coined to describe the unexpectedly low rate of coronary heart disease in France despite the fact the French are known to partake in foods high in saturated fat such as cheese, cream and pastry. Researchers began to search for what else they were consuming that might be protecting their hearts. The French drink a lot of wine, so wine was identified as being a good candidate because of its high antioxidant content. It must be said, however, that lifestyle is important. Studies of drinkers in France have shown those who drink wine in moderation are also less likely to be overweight and more likely to be active and eat a healthy diet. Visitors to Paris will notice for example that Parisians walk a lot (driving in Paris is a health hazard in itself!), almost always take time to enjoy meals, they don't snack much between meals, and they eat smaller portions.

A review of scientific studies concluded that daily consumption of 150 ml (5 fl oz) of wine (that's a little more than ½ cup) reduces cardiovascular disease by 32 per cent.

But wait! Because there are health risks involved in drinking alcohol—especially to excess—it's important to see wine as an enjoyable option in moderation rather than an essential for heart disease protection. The American Heart Association does not suggest you start drinking alcohol in order to reduce your risk of heart disease, but rather if you already drink, to do so in moderation. Drinking excessively is associated with dying young from other causes apart from cardiovascular disease.

What's the best tipple?

In short, the jury is still out about which type of alcoholic drink is best. Alcohol itself, no matter where it comes from, is protective by increasing good HDL cholesterol and 'thinning' the blood. Although some studies show wine to have the protective edge, the sum total of research is inconclusive. If wine does have an edge, and especially red wine, it's probably due to high levels of antioxidants. The polyphenolic antioxidants in red wine have been shown to reduce the oxidation of bad LDL cholesterol, increase good HDL, reduce inflammation, improve flexibility of blood vessels (endothelial function), reduce the sticky-ness of the blood and reduce the risk of clots.

How much is OK to drink?

For protecting your heart, it seems it is not what you drink but HOW you drink it that makes the difference. A little alcohol each day is protective, yet 'binge' drinking, or drinking large amounts less often, is actually harmful. The consensus of health authorities around the world is no more than 2–3 drinks a day for men and 1–2 for women. The National Health and Medical Research Council (NHMRC) of Australia suggests it is risky to drink more than 4 drinks a day for men and more than 2 drinks a day for women. If weight is a problem, then less is best.

Studies indicate 1–2 standard drinks a day is protective against heart disease.

For people with diabetes, drinking small amounts of alcohol is also protective against coronary heart disease, but drinking more than 1 standard drink a day may actually increase the risk. Interestingly, drinking alcohol in moderation helps insulin to work better (improves insulin sensitivity).

The downside

Unfortunately, drinking alcohol can raise triglyceride levels and blood pressure. It is also high in kilojoules and can cause weight gain. Again, limiting how much you drink makes the difference.

What is a standard drink?

100 ml (3½ fl oz) wine/sparkling wine
285 (9½ fl oz) beer (middie)
450 ml (15 fl oz) light (2% alcohol) beer (schooner)
30 ml (1 fl oz, 1 nip) spirits
60 ml (2 flo oz) fortified wine (port, sherry)

How do I enjoy alcohol in moderation?

The trick with alcohol is to enjoy 1–2 a day and no more. This can be challenging, especially if there is social pressure to drink more, or you really like the taste! Try the following ideas to slow down your drinking:

- Have your drinks in smaller, attractive glasses—a glass half full rather than half-empty!
- Drink slowly, taking small mouthfuls with good breaks between mouthfuls to really savour the flavour.
- Pace your eating and drinking at meal times by putting your fork and glass down between mouthfuls and making conversation.
- Alternate your alcoholic drinks with non-alcoholic drinks. If weight is an issue, choose low-kilojoule options such as water (with a slice of lemon or a dash of lime juice), soda water, diet soft drinks and weak cordial.

- Choose light beer.
- Have half-nips of spirits with plenty of ice, with water or mixers.
- In warm weather, mix your white wine with soda—a spritzer.
- Keep your wine glass close to you so as to monitor how often it is refilled.
- Be assertive in controlling how much you drink. A firm 'no thank you' with a smile while placing your hand over your glass is usually effective.
- If you are given too much, don't feel you need to finish it all (same goes for food).
- Pre-mixed drinks can vary in their alcohol content—check the label for the number of standard drinks they contain.
- Sweet pre-mixed drinks can have loads of sugar—avoid/limit these.
- Beware of creamy cocktails as they are very high in alcohol, saturated fat and kilojoules—not very heart-friendly at all.

Did you know?

Cooking wine causes the alcohol to evaporate, but most of the antioxidants remain.

Quickies for 2

Pears Poached in Red Wine

This is a great idea for enjoying the goodness of fruit with the bonus of red wine flavour and antioxidants, but without the alcohol that is evaporated during cooking.

Simmer 2 medium pears, sliced in half lengthways, in ½ cup of red wine, ¼ cup of sugar, 3 cloves and 1 cinnamon stick for around 15 minutes in a covered saucepan, turning to ensure even coating. Serve with a heaped tablespoon of vanilla low fat fromage frais (dairy dessert) and sprinkle with powdered cinnamon.

Sangria Punch

This is a very festive drink that's low in alcohol—1 standard drink per serve. The name sangria is derived from the Spanish word for blood, describing the colour from the red wine.

Mix together ¾ cup red wine, ½ cup chopped orange, lemon, apple and pear, ½ cup diet lemonade or ginger ale and ½ cup pure fruit juice in a jug. Serve over ice in a fancy wine glass garnished with orange slices.

Cooking with wine

Cooking with wine is a great way to add flavour without salt to savoury dishes, and richness without saturated fat to sweet dishes.

- Add some red wine to tomato-based pasta sauce or casseroles.
- Add red wine to marinades for red meats, and white wine for chicken and fish.
- Port is delicious in a gravy or sauce for beef.
- Mirin is Japanese rice wine and is delicious added to Asian-style sauces and dressings.
- White wine is great for seafood soups and risottos.
- Sweet liqueurs add delicious flavour to low fat puddings and desserts.

TIPS WITH WINE

- An opened bottle of wine will last three days if sealed and stored in the fridge—there's no need to finish the bottle! Just pour red wine half an hour before serving to take the chill off.
- A typical bottle of wine (12% alcohol) contains seven standard drinks.
- Glasses of wine served in restaurants, bars and clubs (often those stylish, large glasses) are always more than one standard drink and can be up to three in just one glass.
- Alcoholic drinks should list the number of standard drinks they contain on the label.

Chocolate

What's good about chocolate (besides the obvious!)? Chocolate is made from cocoa beans that are naturally rich in flavonoid antioxidants called procyanidins (catechin and epicatechin). These antioxidants have been shown in scientific studies to reduce oxidation of LDL cholesterol, increase good HDL cholesterol, help blood vessels be more flexible and less stiff (improve endothelial function), prevent the blood becoming 'sticky' and forming clots, and lower blood pressure.

Good quality chocolate is an indulgence food you can feel good about

Chocolate comes in several forms. Cocoa powder contains the most, containing 10 per cent by weight of flavonoids. Next comes dark chocolate, and the higher the cocoa content, the more antioxidants it contains. Milk chocolate contains half as much as dark chocolate, and white chocolate contains no antioxidants. Remember chocolate is high in saturated fat and kilojoules so go easy. Cocoa powder is a delicious way to enjoy chocolate as a drink and contains much less fat than solid chocolate. Enjoying chocolate with nuts is a good way to combine heart-friendly nutrients in an indulgent and enjoyable way.

Different types of chocolate

A good rule of thumb is 'dark and rich' is best.

In terms of antioxidant content, dark chocolate is top of the heart-benefit heirachy tree—high cocoa chocolate contains up to 70% cocoa and the percentage is usually on the label.

BEST: Cocoa powder

GOOD: Dark chocolate (semi-sweet/bitter sweet/high cocoa) are basically the same thing—dark chocolate with no milk solids and than 35–40% cocoa content

GOOD: Drinking chocolate (cocoa + sugar)

OK: Milk chocolate

NOT GOOD: Compound chocolate

NOT GOOD: White chocolate—contains only the cocoa butter and no cocoa solids at all so technically it's not really chocolate.

What about chocolate bars?

Chocolate bars with added ingredients like caramel, nougat, marshmallow and biscuit/wafer are lower in chocolate flavonoids and high in kilojoules. They are also getting bigger in size and more and more widely available. Avoid grabbing these as a quick snack and instead take some time to enjoy a modest portion of rich, dark chocolate in a relaxed way. Many people say dark chocolate is easier to stop eating because its richness and intensity is more satisfying.

What is a serve?

An 'extra' or treat food is suggested as being equivalent to 600kJ by the Australian Guide to Healthy Eating. See page 147 for eating plans and how many extras to have.

A serve of chocolate is around:

25 g (1 oz) chocolate = 6 small squares, ½ small bar.

Enjoy it occasionally or in small portions as a treat. If you are following a kilojoule controlled eating plan, have less than this amount as a treat (around 15 g (½ oz); see page 147 for eating plans.

Case Study: Antioxidants in beverages

Researchers from Cornell University in the US discovered that hot cocoa had a higher total antioxidant capacity than red wine or tea. Hot cocoa had the highest amount of phenolics and flavanoids, followed by red wine, then green tea and black tea.

Can chocolate lower cholesterol?

Chocolate is high in saturated fat, so it's not a cholesterol-lowering food (sorry!). But interestingly chocolate feeding studies have shown that eating chocolate regularly does not increase cholesterol either (where can we sign up to participate?). Forget about eating chocolate to lower cholesterol, but savour it in small portions as an indulgent treat that contains beneficial antioxidants and just for the taste of it!

Quickies

Hearty Hot Chocolate for 2

This recipe is really satisfying on chilly evenings.

Combine 1¾ cups of skim milk or soy milk with 3 tablespoons of cocoa powder, 2 teaspoons of honey and 6 squares (25 g/1 oz) of dark bittersweet/high cocoa chocolate. Heat all ingredients gently until the chocolate is dissolved and sprinkle with sifted cocoa powder. Serve with almond bread or Pistachio, Oat and Almond Biscuits (page 186).

You could make a mocha variation by adding 2 tablespoons of strong coffee. Top with a marshmallow.

Chilli Chocolate Nuts (8 small serves)

The idea of mixing chilli with chocolate is ancient. An exotic and interesting balance of sweet, smooth and hot. The heat from the chilli gives this chocolate extra benefits; antioxidants and it's harder to overeat!

Roast, carefully, ½ cup of unsalted nuts under the grill, such as almonds, cashews, peanuts or hazelnuts. Spread evenly on a sheet of greaseproof paper, and add ¼ cup of puffed rice. Place 100 g (3½ oz) dark semi-sweet/high cocoa chocolate pieces in a ceramic dish and microwave for 1 minute, or until melted. Stir in 1 teaspoon chilli oil with a metal spoon and pour over the nuts and rice. Place any remaining nuts and rice on the top of the chocolate to ensure all are included. Allow to cool. Cut into 8 pieces.

How do I enjoy quality chocolate in moderation?

- Take time to savour your chocolate slowly so as to fully appreciate the mouth-filling flavour and creamy texture.
- Enjoy a small portion of plain dark chocolate or dark chocolate with nuts with a short black (espresso coffee) or small glass of port to finish a meal.
- Enjoy a dark chocolate fondue (melted chocolate and evaporated skim milk) with fruit like strawberries, banana slices and raspberries for an indulgent dessert.
- Make a hot chocolate or iced chocolate using skim milk or soy milk, cocoa powder and a little sugar.
- Add a scoop of cocoa powder to a banana smoothie made on low fat milk or soy milk.
- Sprinkle cocoa powder and a little sugar on hot wholegrain toast with plant sterol spread (a variation on cinnamon toast).
- Sprinkle a combination of grated dark chocolate and roasted slivered almonds over a scoop or two of low fat ice-cream.
- For an indulgent sweet snack on the go, combine dark chocolate pieces with chopped apricots, raisins and hazelnuts.

19: Tea and coffee

Both tea and coffee are derived from plants and therefore contain antioxidants as well as caffeine (a stimulant). They also contribute towards your daily fluid needs. However, you can have too much of a good thing, so balance your tea and coffee with a variety of other beverages, including plenty of water.

Caffeine

Caffeine is found naturally in the leaves, seeds and fruits of over 60 plants, including tea leaves, coffee beans, cocoa beans and guarana. Caffeine has a mild stimulating affect that helps boost alertness, concentration and energy levels, but having too much can cause anxiety, increased blood pressure and sleeping difficulties. Drinking some types of coffee to excess may increase cholesterol levels.

How much caffeine?

More than 300 mg of caffeine a day is considered high, although some international recommendations say up to 400 mg is fine. More than 500 mg is associated with anxiety, irritability, headache and sleep disturbance.

What confuses the issue is that everyone is different in how they tolerate caffeine, with regular users developing greater tolerance. People with high blood pressure, children, adolescents, and the elderly may be more vulnerable to the adverse effects of caffeine. Pregnant women are advised to avoid or limit caffeine intake, and those with reflux may find coffee aggravates their symptoms.

300 mg of caffeine a day is roughly equal to:
*   Four average cups, or three average size mugs, of instant coffee.
*   Three average cups of brewed coffee.
*   Six average cups of tea.

Food/drink	Caffeine (mg)
Tea (250 ml/9 fl oz)	10–50
Instant coffee, 1 tsp in 250 ml (9 floz)	60–80
Decaf instant coffee, 1 tsp (250 ml/9 fl oz)	3
Perc/plunger coffee 1tsp (250 ml/9 fl oz)	60–120
Espresso coffee (1 shot, 30 ml/1 fl oz) used to make long black, cappuccino and latte	100 (av.)
Cola-type soft drinks (1 cup/250 ml/9 fl oz)	36
'Energy' drinks (1½ cups/375 ml/13½ fl oz)	80
Hot chocolate (1 cup/250 ml)	6
Milk chocolate (100 g/3½ oz)	20
Dark chocolate (30 g/1 oz)	20

Source: Adapted from Food Standards Australia & New Zealand. http://www.foodstandards.gov.au/whatsinfood/caffeine/index.cfm

You can enjoy up to two instant coffees (or 1 brewed) AND 4 cups of tea daily without overdoing the caffeine.

The caffeine content of tea and coffee varies a lot according to how it's made. If it tastes strong, then it's likely to contain more caffeine (and also more antioxidants). For example, an espresso tastes quite strong and contains much more caffeine than a cup of instant coffee or tea. The table below gives you a rough idea of caffeine content of foods and drinks.

Caffeine and hydration

Enjoying caffeine-containing drinks like tea and coffee in moderation does not cause dehydration and they can contribute to your daily fluid quota. This is because the diuretic effect is very mild and regular drinkers develop a tolerance.

Is caffeine addictive?

You don't get addicted to caffeine like other drugs such as alcohol or illegal drugs, but if you enjoy tea or coffee regularly, you may notice mild symptoms if you stop, such as headaches, fatigue and irritability.

If you're currently having too much, then cut down gradually.

Tea

Tea is made from the leaves of a plant called *Camellia sinensis*. The leaves are picked and dried to make green or black (regular) tea. Green tea is lightly steamed soon after picking to suspend oxidative changes, while black tea is allowed to oxidise. Oolong tea is made by partial oxidation of the tea leaves. Herb tea is not technically tea at all as it is not made from *Camellia sinensis* but rather herbs, flowers and spices.

> **Both black, green and oolong tea contains flavonoid antioxidants, they are just different types.**
> **Green teas contain more simple flavonoids called catechins, while black tea contains more complex flavonoids called theaflavins and thearubigins.**

Tea and heart disease

A number of population studies have shown that drinking tea is associated with a decreased risk of cardiovascular disease. There are a number of different ways tea is thought to offer this protection, mostly related to the flavonoid antioxidant content.

Flavonoid antioxidants in tea have been shown to reduce the oxidation of bad LDL cholesterol, one of the mechanisms contributing to atherosclerosis or 'hardening' of the arteries. Drinking tea has also been shown to improve the elasticity and flexibility of blood vessels (endothelial function).

There are other things in tea that could also be protective against heart disease. Tea contains the B vitamin folate that reduces homocysteine in the blood—high homocysteine levels are believed to be bad news for heart disease risk. Tea flavonoids can also reduce homocysteine levels. Population studies also link drinking tea with lower blood pressure—another risk factor for heart disease.

Tea and cholesterol

Although it's not 100 per cent proven at this stage, drinking black and green tea has been shown to lower total and bad LDL cholesterol in human studies. Even so, it has enough other benefits to support a role in a heart-friendly eating plan.

How much tea?

The benefits for heart health appear at around 3–4 cups a day in scientific studies. Keep in mind you can drink up to 6 cups of tea without going into the 'high' level for caffeine consumption. However, if you drink coffee as well then you'll need to factor in the caffeine from all your beverages.

Does green tea aid weight loss?

Green tea and the flavonoid antioxidants it contains is by no means a magic bullet for weight loss, but it might have positive effects—especially if you drink it instead of other sweetened drinks and as part of a heart-friendly eating plan.

Green tea has received a lot of media attention because of studies suggesting the catechin antioxidants it contains may help with weight loss. The catechins in green tea are unique and have very long names that are usually shortened, the most well known being EGCG. Experiments with green tea have shown increases in the amount of energy burned and the use of fat as fuel in the body, and better weight and body fat loss. While this sounds promising, more research is needed.

TEA FACTS
- Tea is the second most widely consumed beverage after water in the world.
- The longer tea is left to brew, the higher the flavonoid antioxidant content.
- Adding milk does not affect the antioxidant activity.

What about herbal infusions?

Herbal infusions such as chamomile and peppermint are caffeine free and virtually kilojoule-free when taken without additions. They don't contain the flavonoid antioxidants in tea but they can contribute to daily fluids for hydration.

How do I enjoy tea in moderation?

- Take time to enjoy 'taking tea'.
- Embrace the ceremony of tea by serving in attractive cups.
- If you add milk, ensure it is low fat.
- If you use sugar, gradually use less.

How to make the perfect cuppa

1. Always refill your jug with fresh water rather than reboil old water as this adds oxygen to the water, which improves flavour.
2. When brewing loose-leaf tea in a pot, use 1 rounded teaspoon per person.
3. Allow regular black tea to brew for 3 minutes, green tea for 4 minutes and Oolong tea for 6 minutes.

4. Don't add milk to green tea, Oolong or Lapsang Souchong.
5. Try making loose-leaf tea in a plunger pot (also used to make coffee) and you won't need to use a tea strainer.
6. Don't try to re-use tea leaves—always make a fresh pot with new tea.
7. Visit a tea shop and try new and interesting blends and varieties.
8. For interest and variety, try flavoured black tea.
9. Green tea is an acquired taste but flavoured green tea can be a nice introduction.

TEA TIPS

Store tea in a cool dry place.

Keep loose-leaf tea and tea bags in an airtight container away from other strong smelling foods (such as herbal infusion bags).

What is white tea?

White tea is a premium type of tea also known as silver tip; the unopened buds of new tea leaves.

What is chai?

Chai is tea flavoured with spices and originates from India. It is traditionally served very sweet with lots of milk; however, chai loose-leaf tea and tea bags are now available for you to prepare chai tea with low fat milk and less sugar.

Quickies for 2

Sparkling Green Apple Iced Tea

This is a low sugar, low-kilojoule drink with the goodness of apple and green tea antioxidants.

Steep two green tea bags in 1 cup of hot water for 3–4 minutes. Leave aside to cool. Add 1 cup of unsweetened apple juice and 1 cup of diet lemonade (or soda water for a less sweet result). Serve over ice and a few apple slices and garnish with fresh mint.

DIY Chai Tea

This is a great idea to prepare for afternoon tea on a weekend, or for when friends visit and you want something a bit special (simply double the amounts for 4 people). Serve in fancy china for the full ceremony.

Place 1 cup of prepared strong black tea and 1 cup of skim milk in a saucepan with 1 cinnamon stick (or ¼ teaspoon powdered cinnamon), 1 clove, 1 piece of raw ginger (crushed to release the flavour), 2 cardamom pods (crushed), a pinch of nutmeg, ½ teaspoon vanilla essence and 1 tablespoon brown sugar. Simmer gently for 5 minutes. Pour into cups through a strainer.

Add flavour and flavonoid antioxidants to a fruit compote by making it with tea rather than just water

Coffee

Coffee can be enjoyed in moderation as part of a heart-friendly eating plan. To enjoy the likely benefits without the downsides avoid the 'add-ons' like full cream milk, cakes and biscuits.

From the bush to barista

Coffee beans grow inside a red-coloured berry on the coffee bush. There are two main species, *Robusta* and *Arabica*, with *Arabica* being of higher quality. After harvest, the beans are removed from inside the fleshy fruit and then hulled to leave 'green' coffee beans. The beans are then roasted to fully develop the flavour and aroma, ready for packaging as whole or ground coffee.

What's good about coffee?

Coffee beans contain antioxidants from the polyphenol family, namely chlorogenic and caffeic acids and clinical studies have shown that coffee drinking increases antioxidant activity inside the body. Drinking coffee appears to have health benefits. Regular coffee drinkers have a lower risk of developing gallstones, Parkinson's disease, liver disease, and type 2 diabetes. The research is not entirely clear as to why, but the antioxidants are likely to play a role.

Coffee and cholesterol

Unfiltered boiled coffee contains cafestol and kahweol (diterpenes) that can increase cholesterol levels. Boiled and plunger coffee contains the highest amounts, espresso contains moderate amounts, while instant coffee contains very low amounts. Using filter paper tends to remove these substances, but again the general message is, don't have too much and enjoy coffee in moderation as part of heart-friendly lifestyle.

Coffee and coronary heart disease

Although drinking large amounts of strong coffee is risky for the heart, some coffee appears to be better than drinking none at all for heart disease risk (an effect similar to alcohol).

The beneficial effects for the heart appear to kick-in at 2–3 cups of brewed coffee a day (providing 200–300 mg caffeine), which fits neatly into the generally recommended moderate limit of caffeine intake.

But wait ... The other potential bad news is that coffee consumption may increase blood pressure, homocysteine levels and blood vessel stiffness in the heart, all of which are known to increase the risk of heart disease.

The bottom line is, if you have high blood pressure, you're probably best to err on the side of caution. Enjoy less coffee (1–2 cups brewed coffee a day, providing 100–200 mg caffeine) and focus on healthy living to get it down—less salt and plenty of vegetables, fruit, low fat dairy products and physical activity.

How do I enjoy coffee in moderation?

- Resist the temptation to 'up-size' your coffee—use a regular sized cup and order regular sized servings at cafes.
- Enjoy your coffee less strong (by using less).
- Always ask for low fat milk.
- Use the single shot function of your home espresso machine.
- If you're trying to cut down on caffeine, try decaf.

Watch the extras!

Adding full cream milk, especially in a latte, is not recommended for cholesterol lowering—use skim or low fat milk instead. Adding sugar won't affect your cholesterol, but does add kilojoules, so add as little as you can. The big risk to watch is for high saturated fat treats that tend to go with coffee like biscuits and cakes—limit these to special occasions.

What about decaf?

Drinking decaffeinated coffee is a good way to keep enjoying coffee while trying to cut back on caffeine. 'Decaf' coffee is available as instant, ground and whole beans and has almost all the caffeine removed, leaving around 3 mg per cup.

Quickies for 2

Affogato

Prepare ¼ to ⅓ cup of strong black coffee (2 shots of espresso). Place a scoop of low fat ice-cream in the base of 2 short glasses or small cups and pour half the coffee over the top of each. Serve with a single Italian-style sponge finger biscuit.

Iced Mocha

Prepare ⅓ cup of black coffee. Stir in 2 teaspoons of sugar and 2 tablespoons cocoa powder and allow to cool. Pour half the coffee mixture over ice into two tall glasses. Top up with ⅔ cup skim milk and stir well. Sprinkle with cocoa powder and shavings of dark chocolate.

Low Fat Tiramisu

This is a light twist on a rich Italian classic.

Cut 4 Italian sponge-finger biscuits into pieces and place in the base of two parfait glasses. Pour 1½ tablespoons strong black coffee and 3–4 drops of rum essence over each. Top each with 2 tablespoons of low fat coffee or chocolate yoghurt or dairy dessert and 2 tablespoons of low fat ricotta cheese. Create a swirled effect by dipping and dragging the handle of a fork through the yoghurt and ricotta. Sprinkle with cocoa powder and garnish with fresh strawberries.

Part 3

Eat to beat cholesterol

in your kitchen

20: Getting your kitchen into gear

Your kitchen is the powerhouse of heart-healthy nutrition. To ensure the meals and snacks you produce are the best for lowering your cholesterol and protecting your heart, all the equipment and materials need to be in place to make preparing food easier.

You've heard the adage that a shoddy tradesman always blames his tools, so make sure this doesn't apply to you in your kitchen. Having a good selection of tools and utensils is important for you to produce your best results—healthy food that looks appealing, tastes great and makes you look good in the kitchen!

Knives

Using quality knives and sharpening them regularly will make cooking a breeze. You'll need around 4–5 of different sizes, including a long serrated edge knife for slicing crusty wholegrain bread. Storing your knives in a block, or on a magnetised rack will keep them in top condition and reduces the chances of cutting yourself while rummaging through your kitchen drawers.

Chopping boards

Plastic boards are best because bugs can't hide away in the grain like in wooden ones. Ideally, buy several different coloured boards and allocate separate boards for raw meat/fish/chicken and another for uncooked/raw foods to prevent cross contamination.

Mixing bowls

A set of stainless steel kitchen bowls of different sizes will keep you organised as you cook because you can keep chopped ingredients separate. They're also great for mixing and coating. You'll need a glass, ceramic or pyrex dish for marinating foods.

Pots and pans

Solid-based saucepans with well-fitting lids will help you cook pasta, rice, noodles and couscous like a pro, as well as make sauces. Around 3–4 of varying sizes should do. A steamer attachment will produce moist and tender vegetables and meat, chicken or fish.

A wok is an essential for Asian-style cooking. Stir-frying produces fabulously crisp and colourful vegetables and is marvelously quick and simple. Non-stick frying pans are perfect for healthy pan-frying meat, vegetable and egg recipes.

Microwave

A microwave cooks fast and uses less energy so it's a great time saver. It also preserves nutrients, especially in vegetables. No water is needed, just place vegetables in a microwave cooking container and press go! Have a couple of microwave cooking containers of different sizes. You can also use microwave-safe glass and ceramics in the microwave and these are best for foods that are oilier or sweeter as these can stain plastic cookware.

Measuring

Invest in a set of measuring cups and spoons so you can follow recipes accurately. These also help you stay in control of portion sizes where these are important, such as in oil, pasta and rice. A liquid measuring jug is an essential for measuring liquid ingredients. A set of kitchen scales are also useful. For example, for measuring accurate portions of meat, chicken and fish. After a while you'll have a better understanding of what the right amounts look like and be able to estimate more accurately without weighing.

Gadgets and gizmos

There are some pieces of kitchen equipment that just makes things easier and more fun. A quality can-opener, vegetable peeler, grater and garlic crush are essential. A coffee machine will provide café quality at home, or a coffee plunger can make for a nicer experience than instant coffee. A teapot and china cups also take a 'tea-break' to a whole new level. A juicer can make phyto-chemical-rich vegetable and fruit juices (look for machines which preserve more of the pulp and fibre). Bread lovers, you can bake your own with a bread machine—wholegrain and low sodium mixes are available.

Containers

Good sealable plastic containers that can go from the fridge or freezer to the microwave make food storage safer, prevent mess and smells in your fridge, and allow you to use leftovers wisely—great for the food budget, and saves time. A good lunchbox will keep your food fresh and in good shape to help you enjoy healthier options at work or play. Re-sealable plastic bags also come in handy for nuts and dried fruit. A small screw-top glass jar is excellent for making dressings.

Tableware

Food is meant to be a social and enjoyable experience. If you're serious about eating well, pay attention to your table. What does it say about you? If you've made your mind up to be a healthy person, be kind to yourself and believe that you deserve good health and wellbeing, then you will make time to enjoy your meal in a pleasant setting. Attractive plates, cutlery, glasses and serviettes add to the sense of occasion and add to the enjoyment of your cooking. A little relaxing music is a nice finishing touch, and stopping between mouthfuls to talk is a great way to slow your pace of eating and improve digestion and satisfaction.

Smart cooking

Let's review the 'Heart-friendly Diet'.

1.	5+ vegetables a day
2.	2+ fruit a day
3.	Herbs and spices not salt
4.	2+ wholegrains a day
5.	Low GI foods at most meals
6.	2+ meals a week with legumes
7.	30 g/1 oz nuts most days
8.	2+ fish meals a week
9.	At least 1½+ tablespoons healthy oils and spreads daily
10.	25 g of plant sterol-enriched spread a day
11.	Perhaps 1–2 standard alcoholic drinks daily
12.	Tea and coffee in moderation (Up to 3–4 teas plus 2–3 coffees daily)

Healthy-heart tips for preparing food

To make the most of heart-friendly goodness in vegetables and fruit:

- Leave the skin on where you can.
- Don't leave chopped vegetables in the air too long before cooking.
- Cook with little or no water to preserve vitamins.
- Use quicker cooking methods such as microwaving, stir-frying and steaming.

To remove saturated fat from meat:

- Trim visible fat from meat and chicken before cooking (fish skin is OK).
- Buy leaner cuts such as lean/trim mince.
- Remove the skin from chicken.

To make pulses and legumes less 'windy':

- Discard the water used for soaking dried peas and beans.
- Discard the water in canned legumes, and rinse well.

To keep food safe:

- Store food in the fridge or freezer.
- Keep food well wrapped or covered.
- Defrost food in the fridge or microwave, not on the bench/sink.
- Wash hands and equipment with hot soapy water.
- Keep raw and cooked food in different bowls when cooking in batches.
- Use different utentils and chopping boards for raw

and cooked ingredients.

- Ensure you discard the marinade from raw meat, unless it is to be cooked.
- Always re-heat food until piping hot.

Healthy-heart cooking tips

Reduce saturated fat and kilojoules.

• Use lighter cooking methods such as steaming, microwaving and stir-frying.

• Use non-stick cookware to reduce the need for too much oil.

• Heat the pan a little before adding oil so that it spreads easily and covers the base of the pan.

• Use an oil spray for coating meat and vegetables for roasting.

• Measure oil for stir-frying.

• Roast meats on a rack and separate the fat from the juices and discard.

• Chill soups and casseroles made with meat, skim and discard the fat.

• Use low fat milk and reduced-fat cheese and yoghurt in cooking.

• Use a sterol-enriched margarine spread rather than butter in baking.

• Leave deep-frying for special occasions only (and use a healthy oil such as peanut, olive, canola). Make sure the oil is at the correct temperature and always drain food on absorbent paper towel.

• Use reduced-fat coconut milk and only very occasionally.

The perfectly balanced plate

Use the following dinner plate-guide to make sure you are eating a variety of foods in the right proportions. About half your plate should be filled with vegetables or salad, a quarter with lean meat and a quarter with grain foods (preferably wholegrain) such as pasta, rice or bread. For weight loss, consider using a smaller plate. For bigger appetites, use a bigger plate but the proportion stays the same. It's nutritionally a good idea for a smaller women to use a smaller plate and a larger man to use a larger one—one situation where equality is not the aim!

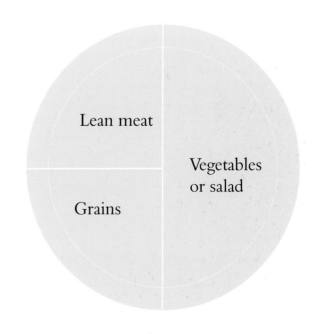

How to beat cholesterol with your favourite recipes

There's no need to do away with your favourite recipes, just make them heart-friendly!

Lasagna:

For white sauce: use sterol-enriched margarine spread instead of butter, low fat milk and reduced-fat cheese; or use ricotta instead of white sauce.

For meat filling: Use extra lean mince and substitute red lentils (or grated vegetables) for ⅓ meat.

Pasta:

Use wholemeal lasagna sheets.

For topping: use reduced fat cheese.

Serve with a salad.

Spaghetti bolognaise:

Use extra lean mince.

Salt-reduced canned tomatoes.

Add red lentils or kidney beans, or grated vegetables.

Use wholemeal spaghetti.

Serve with a salad.

Roast dinner:

Use kangaroo roast, lean lamb roast, lean turkey roast.

Use spray oil on vegetables.

Include a variety of vegetables such as garlic, onion, sweet potato, parsnip, zucchini, pumpkin, squash, capsicum, baby eggplant.

Use reduced-salt gravy powder.

Quiche:

Use filo pastry or brown rice base, or omit pastry (making it a frittata).

Use high omega eggs.

Use salmon in springwater rather than bacon.

Serve a small piece with lots of salad and a slice of wholegrain bread.

Smart shopping in the supermarket
Shop regularly

When you have healthy food on hand, there's less reason to order takeaway. Ensure you shop regularly for fresh ingredients such as vegetables, fruit and dairy, and keep your pantry stocked with dry and canned goods. Meat, chicken and fish can be stored in the freezer—bag into meal sized amounts and take the right amount out when needed. Keep your bread in the freezer and take it out as you need it so it stays fresh. If shopping is a struggle, shop online and have your groceries delivered, or order a weekly box of fruit and vegetables from your greengrocer. Produce markets are very popular so why not make a day of it and select the freshest locally grown food?

21: Eating plans to beat cholesterol

So you're serious about getting your cholesterol down, and it would be good to lose a few kilograms as well. These healthy eating plans provide specific dietary advice to ensure you get results and make the most of all the heart-friendly foods available. You won't feel hungry on our eating plans, as they include breakfast, lunch and dinner with some snack suggestions to keep you going in between. You really do need to eat three meals a day. Skipping meals sets the the perfect trap for snack attacks on all the wrong foods.

Everyone knows that one plan won't suit all—so here are some options depending on whether you are a food lover, a time-poor desperado or a natural born food accountant.

The Cook's Plan:
Two weeks of delicious recipes, quickies and meal ideas that are low in kiloujoules.

The Snatch and Grab Plan:
One week of hand-to-mouth ideas for when time is of the essence and you're hardly in the kitchen.

Let's face it. Many of us lead very busy lives and rely on others to prepare meals and snacks for us. Research suggests we're doing this more than ever before. If you're run off your feet and live hand-to-mouth, don't panic. Choose well and you can still include heart-friendly foods without blowing out on saturated fat. The following weekly eating plan uses takeaway, fast food and restaurant meals as well as other convenient options that will save on time and are still nutritious. If you're careful with portion sizes it will be low in kilojoules (around 6300 kJ/1500 cals). If you need more food, have larger portions.

The DIY Food Plan:
Be your own nutritionist with this DIY food accounting method for nutritionally balanced meals and snacks.

A personal experiment: Visit your doctor for a cholesterol test, follow the plan of your choice for 6 weeks, and then have a repeat test. Losing a little excess weight will boost your result.

If you're a natural born food accountant, you're going to love this plan! Be your own nutritionist and design your own unique eating plan that suits you. Crunch those numbers and count down the days to a lower cholesterol level and a smaller waistline.

The Cook's Plan: first week

DAY	Monday	Tuesday	Wednesday
Breakfast	Banana Walnut Bread 1 serve Skim café latte	1 cup high fibre cereal (with B vitamins and iron) 1 cup of berries 1 tablespoon slivered almonds 1 cup low fat, high calcium milk	2 slices grain and seed toast with 1 tablespoon light plant sterol-enriched spread 1 banana 1 skim caffe latte/hot choc
Lunch	Salmon and Butter Bean Salad with Wholemeal Bread (page 96)	Hummus, Carrot and Baby Spinach Wholemeal Wrap (page 77)	Sardine, Capers, Mint, Lemon, Rocket (arugula), on Rye with Tomatoes (page 196)
Dinner	Cauliflower, Pea and Potato Curry (page 48) with ½ cup steamed brown rice	Oregano Lamb, Risoni and Borlotti Beans with a Fennel, Olive and Zucchini Salad (page 209)	Tandoori Chicken with Yoghurt Sauce and a Lettuce, Tomato, Cucumber, Mint and Mango Salad (page 216)
Dessert/ Snack	1 orange or 2 small mandarins 6 dried apricot halves 1 cup low fat, high calcium milk with 2 teaspoons instant chocolate drink powder	2 nectarines 200g low fat yoghurt	2 kiwi fruit or handful of grapes 1 cup low fat high calcium milk with 2 teaspoons instant chocolate drink powder

Nutrition notes

* Low-kilojoule, approximately 6000–6500kJ (1500–1550cals).

* Snacks can be enjoyed at anytime, either between meals or as dessert.

* A soluble fibre supplement containing psyllium or guar gum is recommended to boost cholesterol lowering.

Thursday	Friday	Saturday	Sunday
Berry Yoghurt Shake (page 172)	1/3 cup raw oats made into porridge with 1 cup low fat, high calcium milk and 2 teaspoons LSA mix 3 prunes	1 thick slice of grain and fruit toast with 3 teaspoons peanut butter (no added salt) Skim caffe latte/hot chocolate	Buckwheat, Lentil and Chive Corncakes with Red Capsicum (Pepper) Salsa and Avocado (page 173)
Chilli Bean Melt (page 77)	Grilled Beef Open Turkish (page 105)	Fish fill-all Flat Bread Wrap (page 96)	Egg, Rocket, Beetroot and Hazelnut Salad (page 100) 2 slices wholegrain bread spread with 1 tablespoon light plant sterol spread
Beef, Creamy Mushroom and Broccolini Penne with a Mixed Leaf Salad (page 208)	Smoked Paprika Chicken and Corn Frittata with Cos and Capsicum Salad (page 202) 2 slices wholegrain bread with 1 tablespoon light plant sterol spread	Roast Pork, Pears and Vegetables with Creamed Parmesan Barley and Cauliflower (page 226)	Barbecued Fish Broccoli and green bean salad (page 44) with a Vinaigrette Dressing (page 41) Sweet Potato Wedges (page 47)
Popcorn, Almond and Pumpkin Kernels, Paw Paw and Pineapple mix (page 180) 1 apple or peach	Saucy Chocolate and Almond Puddings with Raspberries (page 237) 2 kiwi fruit or small mango 1 glass low fat, high calcium milk	Carrot, capsicum and zucchini sticks with Indian yoghurt dip (page 121) Apples topped with Scrunched Filo and Maple Syrup Glazed Brazil Nuts (page 240) 1 cup melon pieces or grapes	Anise Infused Rice Custard with Blood Orange (page 242) 100 g low fat yoghurt 1/2 cup berries

* Ensure you drink 2 litres of fluid daily. Include plenty of water and up to 4 cups of tea and 1 espresso coffee (no sugar with a little reduced-fat milk and sweetener if desired).

* This low-kilojoule eating plan may not be adequate in some vitamins and minerals for people with higher nutritional needs. An Accredited Practising Dietitian (APD) can assess your needs and tailor a plan especially for you.

The Cook's Plan: second week

DAY	Monday	Tuesday	Wednesday
Breakfast	Bircher Muesli (page 72)	Puffed Wheat, Soy Flakes, Oats, LSA and Walnut Cereal, yoghurt, fruit and milk (page 170)	Soy-Good Breakfast (page 80)
Lunch	Crusty Grain Roll with 1 tablespoon light plant sterol spread with 40 g shaved lean roast beef Apple and pistachio salad (page 60)	Mixed grain lemon and dill salmon salad sandwiches (page 96)	Tuna and Cracked Wheat Salad (page 193) 1 light pita bread with 1 tablespoon light plant sterol spread
Dinner	Barbecued Chicken, Corn Cobs and Potato and Baby Beet Salad (page 215)	Warm Beef Salad with Lime, Sweet Chilli and Herb Dressing (page 210) 1 slice bread with light plant sterol spread	Middle Eastern Chicken and Vegetable Skewers (page 65) Red Cabbage, Orange and Almond Salad (page 86)
Dessert/ Snack	Blueberry, Bran and LSA Muffins (page 188) spread with light plant sterol spread 1 glass of low fat, high calcium milk 1 cup pineapple or 2 kiwi fruit.	1 skim latte/hot chocolate 1 pear or 1 cup melon pieces	Pistachio, Oat and Almond Biscuits (page 186) 1 cup fruit salad Skim caffe latte

Nutrition notes

* Snacks can be enjoyed at anytime either between meals or as dessert.

* Ensure you drink 2 litres of fluid daily. Include plenty of water and up to 4 cups of tea and 1 espresso coffee (no sugar) with a little reduced fat-milk and sweetener if desired.

Thursday	Friday	Saturday	Sunday
Linseed, Rice, Oat Raisin and Apricot Porridge (page 71) 1 cup low fat, high calcium milk or low fat soy milk	2 slices mixed grain and seed toast with 1 tablespoon light plant sterol spread, 1 table-spoon berry fruit spread, Skim caffe latte/hot chocolate made with low fat, high calcium milk	Egg, Beans and Mushrooms on Mixed Grain Muffins (page 171) with ½ cup baby spinach leaves and 2 grilled tomato halves DIY chai (page 133)	1 toasted wholemeal English muffin with 1 tablespoon light plant sterol spread and 1 banana hot chocolate made with low fat-high calcium milk
Pureed Lentil and Vegetable Soup (page 65) 1 slice wholegrain toast with 3 teaspoons light plant sterol spread	Thai Lime Tofu and Noodle Salad (page 55)	Beef and Soba Noodle Soup with Asian Greens and Mushrooms (page 192)	Barbecued Chermoula Lamb, Pumpkin and Eggplant Burghul with Yoghurt and Coriander (page 212) with 1 cup steamed/microwaved broccoli
Steak with Grilled Capsicums, Mushroom and Dill Roasted Buckwheat (page 218)	Spiced Tomato and Butter Bean Spirals with Yellow Capsicum Salad (page 225)	Dill Risotto with Chargrilled Salmon and Asparagus, Baby Carrots and Aioli (page 220)	Fish, Tomato, Saffron and White Bean Soup (page 194)
Iced Mocha (page 135) 1 orange or 2 mandarins	Chilli Chocolate Nuts (page 128) 1 cup berries 1 cup raw snow peas and cap-sicum strips	Orange and Dried Fruit Salad with Orange Liqueur Yoghurt and an Orange, Mint and Liqueur Shot (page 239)	1 cup rockmelon 100 g low fat yoghurt 2 teaspoons walnut pieces

*This low-kilojoule eating plan may not be adequate in some vitamins and minerals for people with higher nutritional needs. An Accredited Practising Dietitian (APD) can assess your needs and tailor a plan especially for you.

The Snatch and Grab Plan (see page 154 for Snatch and Grab Plan Nutrition notes)

DAY	Monday	Tuesday	Wednesday
	Back to work TV night at home	Brekky at work Exercise class after work	Brekky at home
Breakfast	1 cup high fibre cereal with added B vitamins, iron and folate 1 cup low fat, high calcium milk Berries	2 slices wholemeal fruit toast with 1 tablespoon plant sterol spread 1 small skim caffe latte (1 cup)	Tub of prepared bircher muesli Skim hot chocolate (small)
Lunch	(packed from home) 40 g leftover roast beef/kangaroo on a wholemeal flat bread with barley + 1 tablespoon light plant sterol spread 1 cup mixed dark leaf salad	(takeaway) 2 sushi rolls with salmon & avocado Small mixed vegetable and fruit juice (1 cup)	(takeaway) Small container of vegetable and tomato pasta 1 small container of mixed green salad
Dinner	(heat-and-eat) Frozen low fat meal with fish, 1½ cups microwaved frozen mixed vegetables	(takeaway) 1½ cups Thai chilli beef and vegetable stir fry ½ cup steamed rice	(assemble and serve) takeaway barbecue chicken breast (no skin) Microwaved frozen corn cob, peas and broccoli 1 slice wholegrain bread with light plant sterol spread
Dessert/ Snack	1 apple or 1 cup of grapes 40 g pack of mixed nuts and dried fruit	1 cup melon slices 2 wholegrain crispbread with 2 teaspoons light plant sterol spread and fresh tomato and basil 200 ml low fat flavoured milk	1 orange or 2 small mandarins 15 g unsalted nuts 3 dried apricots

Thursday	Friday	Saturday	Sunday
Brekky on the way to work, late night shopping	Night on the town	Out and about DVD night	Entertaining at home
Skim banana smoothie High fibre cereal bar/muesli bar	1½ cups bran flakes with added vitamins and iron 1 cup low fat, high calcium milk ½ cup frozen mixed berries Skim caffe latte (café)	Buckwheat pancakes with berries and 100 g low fat yoghurt Skim hot chocolate	1 slice smoked salmon, 1 high omega poached egg and ½ cup spinach on 2 wholemeal toast with 1 tablespoon light plant sterol spread, 120ml fresh squeezed orange juice and 200ml mineral water Skim caffe latte
(takeaway) Wholemeal roll with avocado, canned salmon and salad	Stir-fry seafood and vegetables with noodles	(takeaway) Grilled fish fillet and salad with lemon Small mixed vegetable and fruit juice	(DIY over the newspaper) Wholegrain sandwich with 1 tablespoon light plant sterol spread, ¼ cup low fat ricotta cheese, grated carrot, chopped capsicum and sultanas
(fast food) 1 vege-burger 1 mixed green salad 1 small fruit juice	(restaurant) 150 g cooked lean steak (no creamy sauces) Steamed vegetables (no butter) Side salad with dressing 1 glass of wine Coffee and 2 petite four chocolates/after dinner mints	(takeaway) 1½ cups stir-fry vegetables and tofu with cashews 1 cup steamed rice	(barbecue at home) 150 g cooked kangaroo/lean beef mini roast ½ cup Sweet Potato Wedges (page 47) Baby spinach leaves, baby beet, spring onion and pine nut salad with canola oil vinaigrette. 1 glass red wine
1 pear or 2 plums 1 small serve low fat frozen yoghurt 1 small bag plain popcorn	15 g walnuts 1 orange or 2 mandarins	(takeaway) Fruit salad and low fat yoghurt (small serve) 25 g dark chocolate with almonds	1 scoop low fat ice-cream with ¼ cup canned berries

The Snatch and Grab Plan

Nutrition notes (see previous page)

* Ensure you drink 2 litres of fluid daily. Include plenty of water and up to 4 cups of tea and 1 espresso coffee (no sugar) with a little reduced-fat milk and sweetener if desired.

* A soluble fibre supplement containing psyllium or guar gum is recommended to boost cholesterol lowering

* This meal plan may not be adequate in some vitamins and minerals for some people with higher nutritional needs. You can consult an Accredited Practising Dietitian (APD) to have a eating plan individualised for you.

A word of warning

Sodium is really difficult to avoid when you're not doing the cooking. Restaurant, takeaway and fast food is generally much higher in sodium, and this plan will contain much more than ideal 1600 mg per day recommended for heart disease risk reduction. If you have high blood pressure, the Snatch and Grab Plan is not the best way to go for any length of time.

The DIY Food Plan
Your energy needs

Energy (kilojoule) needs vary from person to person, however, typical daily kilojoule needs for adults of average weight with moderate levels of physical activity aged 31–50 years are approximately:

Men   11,900 kilojoules (2840 calories)
Women 9,000 kilojoules (2150 calories)

You will need more if:

You are under 30 years old
You are taller than average
You are heavy
You are very active

You will need less if:

You are over 50 years old
You are shorter than average
You are slim
You are inactive
You want to lose weight

How to put together your DIY Food Plan

1. Match your daily kilojoule needs to the energy column in the table. If you need to lose weight, reduce kilojoules by 1000-2000 (250-500 cals).
2. Determine how many serves of each food group to eat each day.
3. Sort the serves of food into meals and snacks in a way that suits you.

Example daily menu for cholesterol lowering—low in kilojoules

Breakfast

1½ cups (50 g/1¾ oz) high fibre breakfast cereal flakes (with added vitamins, folate, iron)

1 cup of reduced-fat, high calcium milk

1 cup strawberries or other berries (flavour with a little sugar/honey or low-kilojoule sweetener if required)

Lunch

Mixed Grain Lemon and Dill Salmon Salad Sandwiches (see page 96)

Dinner

Chilli and Garlic Beef and Vegetable Stir-fry (see page 105)

Snacks/dessert

15 g (½ oz) almonds

1 cup fruit salad pieces

Yoghurt Dip with Crushed Garlic, Cucumber and Mint (see page 121) with

1½ cup of raw vegetables—carrot, cherry tomato, capsicum

Drinks

Ensure around 2 litres of fluid daily. Include plenty of water and up to

4 cups of tea and 1 espresso coffee (no sugar) with a little reduced-fat milk and sweetener if desired.

On target nutrition information		Nutrition notes
Kilojoules	6276 kJ (1500cals)	A soluble fibre supplement containing psyllium (e.g. metamucilTM) or guar gum (e.g. BenefiberTM) is suggested to boost cholesterol lowering. A calcium supplement with vitamin D (200IU or 5ug vitamin D3, cholecalciferol) may be beneficial for those aged over 70 years to meet additional requirements for bone health.
Fat	58 g (34%kJ)	
Polyunsaturated fat	16 g (10%kJ)	
Saturated fat	13 g (8%)	
P:S ratio	1.2	
Cholesterol	161 mg	
Sodium	1271 mg	
Fibre	38 g	

Example daily menu for cholesterol lowering—moderate in kilojoules

Breakfast

1 cup high fibre cereal flakes (with added B vitamins and iron) + ½ cup muesli with
1 cup of low fat milk, 1 cup fruit salad pieces
1 skim café latte

Lunch

Sardine, Chickpea, Kumara, Spinach and Orange Salad (see page 96), 1 cup low fat milk

Dinner

Meat with Herb and Garlic Vegetable Pasta (see page 105)
1 small glass (100 ml/3½ fl oz) red wine

Snacks/Dessert

15 g (½ oz) almonds
1 apple or 2 nectarines
200 g (7 oz) low fat yoghurt

Drinks

Ensure around 2 litres of fluid daily. Include plenty of water and up to 4 cups of tea and 1 espresso coffee
(no sugar) with a little reduced-fat milk and sweetener if desired.

On target nutrition information		Nutrition notes
Kilojoules	9036 kJ (2158 cal)	
Fat	65 g (27%)	A calcium supplement with vitamin D (200IU or 5ug vitamin D3, cholecalciferol) may be beneficial for those aged over 70 years to meet additional requirements for bone health
Polyunsaturated fat	19 g (8%)	
Saturated fat	15 g (6%)	
P: S ratio	1.2	
Cholesterol	200 mg	
Sodium	1482 mg	
Fibre	50 g	

Eating Out

Food on the go—work lunches

While most people agree that eating a healthy lunch is important, one in three Australians skip it at least once a week, and one in 10 rarely or never have it according to a recent poll. 'Too busy' is the main catch-cry of lunch-skippers. But taking a bit of time to eat lunch is critical to maintaining health, controlling weight, boosting energy and concentration levels and simply feeling better overall.

Lunch doesn't need to be a big meal. But you need to choose a food from each group—grains, meat or fish, vegetables and fruit. Of course it's better to make your own lunch because then you know exactly what's in it, but life gets busy and buying your lunch out and about is an inevitable part of modern living. Choose wisely and you can still keep your cholesterol down, look after your heart and keep your waistline in check.

Size matters

A big let-down for many takeaway lunch options is the large portions. For most of us who sit at a desk the extra kilojoules aren't needed and simply go into storage as body fat. Here are two tips:

• Keep your portions modest. Order smaller options, or leave some food behind.
• Try to ignore the voice in your head saying you need to finish everything on your plate. This wisdom was timely in the days of food scarcity but is a shortcut to obesity in this age of abundance.

What to look for

Priorities when choosing takeaway lunches are to minimise saturated fat and kilojoules and maximise heart-friendly foods such as vegetables, fruit, wholegrains, legumes, nuts and seeds and fish. Anything fried, in pastry or a creamy sauce, or covered in cheese is not a good option. Foods with wholegrain bread, rice, vegetables or salad, and beans are a better choice. Because of the increasing awareness about nutrition and health in the community there are healthier fast food choices available.

Sodium alert

Takeaway foods almost always contain too much salt. Help control this by saying no when asked if you want salt added to your food, as is typical is a sandwich shop for example.

Think about drinks

The kilojoules from sugary drinks can really add up (a standard 375 ml/12½ fl oz can of soft drink contains up to 48 g/1¾ oz of sugar—that is 12 teaspoons). Stick to water or diet soft drinks to go with your lunch—or a cup of tea or coffee. Consider boosting your vitamins and antioxidants with a small mixed vegetable and fruit juice (try carrot, orange and ginger), or a sweet finish that's good for you with a flavoured low fat milk, skim milkshake or smoothie.

Lunches to limit	Healthier lunches	Tips
Focaccia	Wholemeal salad roll	Include salmon for omega-3
Schnitzel sandwich	Chicken breast sandwich	Include plenty of salad
Creamy pasta (e.g. carbonara)	Tomato-based pasta sauce	Sauce with vegetables (e g primavera) or seafood (e.g. marinara)
Meat pie/sausage roll	Filled potato with beans or creamed corn and tuna	Skip the cheese and sour cream
Tacos/nachos	Tortilla (e.g. burrito) with bean filling	Skip the cheese and sour cream
Fish and chips	Grilled fish and salad	Add lemon juice and a little mayonnaise
Burger with egg, bacon and cheese	Plain burger (lean is best) with salad or steak sandwich	Skip the bacon, egg and cheese
Indian creamy curry (with coconut)	Tandoori chicken (no skin)	With steamed rice and dahl (lentils)
Thai creamy curry	Stir-fry with vegetables and steamed rice	Seafood stir-fry for omega-3 Tofu stir-fry for soy protein
Thai fried spring rolls/curry puffs	Thai beef and vegetable salad	Steamed rice on the side
Crepe with cheesy filling	Wrap with salad	Include tuna or salmon for omega-3
Doner kebab	Falafel wrap chilli sauce and tabouli	Skip the cheese
Chips and gravy	Sushi rolls or sushi box	Include salmon or tuna for omega-3 Use very little (salty) soy sauce
Quiche (pastry)	Frittata and salad	Vegetable or salmon filling
Creamy soup	Minestrone soup	With wholemeal bread
Spring rolls (fried)	Rice paper rolls	Chilli dipping sauce
Pizza (meat)	Vegetable, bean or seafood	Thin crust is lower in kilojoules Skip the garlic bread
Fried chicken	Barbecue chicken (no skin) or Chicken breast fillet burger	With wholemeal bread, corn and peas
Ice-cream	Low fat yoghurt	Small serving
Cake	Fruit salad	

Café society

Meeting for coffee has become common, and the choice of hot and cold drinks and sweet treats to go with them has exploded. Beware of highly sweetened regular-fat milk drinks with cream on top (hot or cold), and remember there is 10 g of fat per cup of regular fat milk and close to zero in the same amount of skim milk. There are virtually no kilojoules in a cup of black tea or coffee with no sugar (or sweetener instead), and a dash of low fat milk won't break the kilojoule budget. Resist the high fat cakes, slices biscuits, muffins and donuts on display (often over-sized). If you do decide to treat yourself, go for small portions. Biscotti, almond bread or scones (minus the butter and cream) are lighter café treats.

Eating out—restaurants and cafés

If you eat out occasionally as a special treat you can afford to order whatever takes your fancy and it won't make any difference to your health. However, if, like many people, eating out is a regular occurrence (several nights a week), the choices you make are more important.

10 tips for frequent diners

1. Avoid arriving over-hungry—have a healthy snack such as a small handful of nuts or a low fat milk or yoghurt to take the edge off your appetite.
2. Exercise portion caution. Restaurant portions are often too big for many of us, so order small. Try an entrée size main and limit yourself to two modest courses.
3. Ensure you order extra vegetables or salad— standard accompaniments are not usually enough.
4. Alcoholic drinks are often larger than a standard drink—limit yourself to one or two.
5. Order some water and drink this to quench your thirst and to pace yourself between mouthfuls.
6. Relax and eat slowly—make time for conversation.
7. Skip the bread (unless it is wholegrain and then stop at one plain piece) and avoid butter.
8. Avoid fried foods, pastry and rich sauces.
9. Ask staff how dishes are prepared and request no butter or cream.
10. If you have dessert, choose fruit or gelato, share a dessert, or skip straight to coffee/tea.

Multicultural dining

Choose options that are lower in saturated fat and salt.

- Sharing is a popular way to enjoy international cuisine but a good way to lose track of how much you've eaten. Serve yourself once only to avoid overeating.
- Order extra vegetables or salad.
- Order entree size nice pasta dishes.
- Consider vegetarian options.

	Dishes to limit	Healthier options
Italian	Garlic bread	Plain bread, bruschetta
	Salami antipasto	Tuna/beef carpcaccio (raw, thinly sliced)
	Lasagna/parmigiana	Grilled fish and vegetables
	Cannelloni	Minestrone soup
	Pizza/saltimbocca	Ravioli with tomato sauce
	Pasta carbonara (creamy sauce)	Pasta Napolitana (tomato sauce)
	Cheese/creamy risotto	Vegetable risotto
	Tiramisu	Gelato or biscotti
Chinese	Dims sims, spring rolls, prawn toasts, prawn crackers (fried)	Satay sticks, chicken and corn soup, steamed dim sum
	Pork and duck	Seafood, chicken and tofu dishes
	Sweet and sour, honey, satay, plum sauces	Chilli, curry, braised, Szechwan, barbecue or stir-fry
	Omelette, crispy skin chicken	Stir-fry chicken and almonds/cashews
	Fried rice/noodles	Steamed rice
	Sweet and sour fish	Steamed fish
Thai	Soups with coconut milk (e.g. Tom Kha Gai)	Hot and sour soups (e.g. Tom Yum)
	Spring rolls /Curry puffs/money bags	Barbecue octopus, rice paper rolls
	Creamy curries (with coconut milk) e.g. green, red, Massaman, Penang,	Dry curries, Stir-fries with garlic, chilli, ginger, basil
	Chicken wings (fried)	Satay chicken or tofu sticks (go easy on the sauce), beef/chicken salad
	Fried rice/fried noodles (e.g. pad Thai, mee grob) coconut rice	Steamed rice
	Duck	Seafood, chicken, tofu
Lebanese	Entrees in pastry (eg Sambusek, meat cigar/ladies fingers)	Dips and Lebanese bread
	Fried entrees (mezza) e.g. chicken wings	Vine leaves, baked kibbi, stuffed cabbage leaves, (jawaneh), broadbeans (foulia)
	Sausage (e.g. Soujouk, Makanek)	Tabouleh salad, fatouche salad, pilaf, pickled vegetables (kabeece), green beans in tomato sauce (loubyeh)

EATING OUT	Dishes to limit	Healthier options
Lebanese cont.	Lamb meat balls (e.g. kafta)	Meat skewer (Shish kebab, shawourma), skewers with prawn (mishwee) or grilled chicken (shishtawook)
	Fried eggplant, fried cauliflower	Grilled fish, lentil and rice pilaf (mjadra)
	Sweet pastries (e.g. baklava,) and biscuits	Fruit, Turkish delight
Greek	Spinach and cheese triangles (spanakopita)	Greek salad, bread and dips, stuffed vine leaves (dolmades)
	Egg and cheese pastry (tyropita)	Lima beans (gigandes)
	Fried cheese (saganaki, haloumi)	Legumes (fassolia)
	Fried whitebait	Grilled prawns
	Fried calamari	Chargrilled octopus
	Meat or eggplant moussaka	Vegetable and meat skewers (souvlakia)
	Pork sausage (Loukaniko)	Chargrilled lamb, pork or chicken (tis skaras)
	Stuffed eggplant in bechamel sauce	Stuffed vegetables (dolmos)
		Broiled fish (Plaki)
	Sweet pastries (Loukoumathes), biscuits (kourambiie) and cakes	Fruit or yoghurt or Turkish delight (Loukoumi)
Indian	Fried samosa, bhajia, pakora, bondas	Tandoori chicken, chicken tikka, fish tikka
	Flavoured naan (e.g. cheese filled), roti, poori, bhatura, parratha breads, pappadum	Plain naan, chapatti, wholemeal roti
	Pilaf/pilau (fried rice)	Steamed rice
	Pork	Lentil, chick pea, prawn, chicken, vegetable
	Korma, passanda, massala sauces ('wet' curries)	Tandoori or madras, dry curries
	Butter chicken, beef curry	Dahl (lentils), potato curry
	Tandoori lamb	Tandoori chicken or fish
	Lamb biryani	Rogan josh, madras, tikka with prawns, chicken or vegetables
	Pork vindaloo	Chilli or pepper chicken

22: Cooking to beat cholesterol

In order to lower your cholesterol, we've put together recipes that you'll love eating because we believe that enjoying food is an essential for a happy life. Sharing delicious food with those you love is a great way to boost your wellbeing.

About the recipes
Adventure

Food should be fun! We are lucky enough to enjoy an incredible variety of foods and cuisines from around the world. Enjoying foods and ingredients from different cultures is like taking a holiday at your dining table. We encourage you to try new and interesting ingredients and flavours, and we explain what to do with them in simple terms. The added bonus is they're good for you!

Convenience

We realise that many people lead full and busy lives and don't have a lot of time to cook, so we've kept the cooking and preparation times short for most recipes. We acknowledge the role of convenience foods such as canned foods and curry pastes in getting dinner on the table in quick time. If there is a health implication to using these, we point you in the right direction toward healthier options. If you can't get hold of ingredients that are a bit different or exotic, we give you an alternative. We have given the speedy option of microwave cooking for some recipes, and also offer a conventional cooking alternative.

Information

We've provided plenty of information for you to ensure the recipes turn out every time. We've included both metric and imperial weights, as well as household measures to make preparing tour ingredients a breeze. We've allowed for a variety of skill levels and cooking experience, and explained the method in simple terms. If there's anything a bit tricky, we've included a 'Cook's tip' to help you produce a fabulous end result.

Why the recipes are healthy

When you have high cholesterol levels, you don't get any more time in the day to think through how you're meant to achieve all the nutritional targets, so we've done the work for you. Our recipes are complete balanced meals and contain heart-friendly ingredients you've read about in earlier chapters. All the calculations have been done to ensure the recipes are low in saturated fat, cholesterol and sodium and contain an appropriate number of kilojoules (calories) for the eating occasion.

If you're not into technical stuff, then flick over the next section and straight to the recipes…

Nutrition

You'll find 'Nutrition information per serve' for each recipe if you'd like to keep track. There are complete daily eating plans on page 147 if you'd like to put our recipes together as part of controlled eating plan. We've used nutrient tags to help you identify recipes with particular characteristics. For example, if you want to lose weight you can watch out for 'Low kilojoule' tags, and if you're cutting back on sodium to reduce blood pressure you can look for 'Low sodium' tags.

Nutrient tag	When it is used
Low-kilojoule	Main meal 2000 kJ or less Light meal 1500 kJ or less Snack 600 kJ or less
Fibre	Main meal 8 g or more Light meal 6 g or more Snack 4 g or more
Low Sodium	Less than 120 mg/100 g AND Main meal 500 mg or less Light meal 300 mg or less Snack 50 mg or less
Omega-3 (long chain from fish) DHA & EPA	*Excellent* source contains 900 mg per 100 g or more *Great* source contains 250–900 mg per 100 g *Good* source contains 250 mg per 100 g or less
*GI rating**	In low GI recipes, the predominant carbohydrate ingredient(s) is/are low GI

*estimated by GI expert, Dr Susanna Holt

23: Breakfast and brunch

Puffed Wheat, Soy Flakes, Oats, LSA and Walnut Cereal
Low kilojoule, low sodium, low–medium GI

This cereal recipe includes only heart-friendly ingredients and delivers a great tasting combination of crunch, puff and soft textures. The proportions of each ingredient can be changed to taste and it is great as a quick snack anytime. If you can't find soy flakes, try using high fibre, low GI wheat flakes.

Preparation time: 5 minutes
Cooking time: 10 minutes
Storage time: 1 week in an airtight container
Makes: 3½ cups (7 serves)

> ½ cup (60 g/2¼ oz) walnut pieces
> 1 cup (30 g/1 oz) puffed wheat
> 1 cup (55 g/2 oz) soy flakes
> ½ cup (50 g/1¾ oz) traditional rolled oats
> ½ cup (60 g/2¼ oz) LSA (linseed, sunflower and almond blend)
> 2 teaspoons ground cinnamon

Preheat oven to cool 150°C (300°F/Gas Mark 2). Spread the walnuts on a baking tray and bake for 6–8 minutes or until lightly golden. Cool.
Meanwhile, place the puffed wheat, soy flakes, oats, LSA and cinnamon into an airtight cereal storage container. Add the cooled walnut pieces and shake to combine.

Shake container well before serving to make sure you get a taste of all the flavours and textures.

Nutrition note: Look for wholegrain rolled oats, commonly labelled traditional rolled oats, rather than instant or quick oats, as they have a lower GI. You could also use rolled barley, which is also low GI.

Cook's Tips
Try different nuts such as pecans or almonds.
Try adding some dried fruits such as pear, apple, apricots or raisins.
Try adding a soy flake cereal that has dried fruits or nuts added.

Nutrition per serve	
Energy kJ (cals)	727 (173)
Protein	8 g
Total fat	10.8g
Saturated fat	0.9 g
Fibre	4.1 g
Carbohydrate	11.6 g
Cholesterol	0 mg
Sodium	4 mg

Egg, Beans and Mushrooms on Mixed Grain Muffins
High fibre, low GI

A mixed-grain English muffin was used for this recipe. The grains were kibbled rye, kibbled wheat, linseed, linola seed, kibbled corn, sunflower kernels, triticale, kibbled barley and rolled oats—an excellent way of enjoying a variety of healthy grains in the diet.

Preparation time: 5 minutes
Cooking time: 10 minutes
Serves: 2

3 teaspoons sunflower oil
2 x 60 g/2¼ oz flat mushrooms, trimmed
½ cup (150 g/5½ oz) salt-reduced baked
  beans in tomato sauce
2 x 50 g/1¾ oz eggs
2 x 60 g/2¼ oz mixed wholegrain muffins
1 tablespoon light plant sterol spread
2 teaspoons chopped flat leaf parsley

Heat the oil in a non-stick pan over a medium heat. Cook the mushrooms, stem side down until golden, 2–3 minutes, turn and cook the other side. Spoon the baked beans into the tops of the mushrooms to heat while the mushrooms are cooking.

Add the eggs to the pan and cook to liking or poach in a separate pan.

Toast the muffins and spread with plant sterol spread. Serve the mushroom and beans on one half of the muffin and the egg on the other. Sprinkle with parsley.

Nutrition note: This is a good example of a recipe that is higher in fat, but as a breakfast meal is still low in saturated fat. If you're watching your weight, kilojoules are the most important thing to limit and the kilojoules in this recipe are on target (between 1500–2000kJ)

Nutrition per serve	
Energy kJ (cals)	1484 (354)
Protein	18 g
Total fat	17 g
Saturated fat	3 g
Fibre	8 g
Carbohydrate	32 g
Cholesterol	188 mg
Sodium	442 mg

Cereal, Yoghurt, Fruit and Milk
Low kilojoule, low sodium, low–medium GI

Keep a measuring cup in the cereal container for portion control and quick measuring when you are trying to tackle the early morning breakfast rush—the perfect guarantee of the recommended serve and a heart-healthy start to the day.

Preparation time: 5 minutes
Serves: 2

- 1 cup (30 g/1 oz) Puffed Wheat, Soy Flakes, Oats, LSA and Walnut Cereal (see page 170)
- ½ cup (125 g/4½ oz) low fat yoghurt
- 2 x 150 g/5½ oz apples, chopped
- ½ cup (125 ml/4 fl oz) low fat milk (semi-skimmed) or soy milk

Divide cereal between two bowls. Top with yoghurt and apple. Pour on the milk.

Nutrition per serve	
Energy kJ (cals)	1002 (240)
Protein	11 g
Total fat	5.8 g
Saturated fat	0.6 g
Fibre	5 g
Carbohydrate	36 g
Cholesterol	6.5 g
Sodium	92 mg

Berry Yoghurt Shake with Cinnamon Sugar and Cocoa Topping
Low kilojoule, low GI

Preparation time: 3 minutes
Blending time: 2 minutes
Serves: 2

Shake
- 1 cup (250ml/9 fl oz) low fat or soy milk
- ¾ cup (185g/6½ oz) low fat vanilla yoghurt
- ½ cup (80 g/2 ¾ oz) diced strawberries
- ¼ cup (30 g/1 oz) LSA (soy, linseed, sunflower and almond blend)

Topping
- ¾ teaspoon ground cinnamon
- ½ teaspoon sugar
- ¼ teaspoon cocoa powder

Place milk, yoghurt, strawberries and LSA into a blender. Blend for 1–2 minutes. Pour into glasses. Mix together the cinnamon, sugar and cocoa in a small bowl and sprinkle on the shake.

Nutrition per serve	
Energy kJ (cals)	915 (218)
Protein	15.4 g
Total fat	7 g
Saturated fat	0.9 g
Fibre	3.7g
Carbohydrate	24 g
Cholesterol	11 mg
Sodium	154 mg

Buckwheat, Lentil and Chive Corncakes with Red Capsicum (Pepper) Salsa and Avocado

Low kilojoule, low GI

It's always fun making up a batch of hotcakes. These corncakes are a variation to the traditional hotcake and are made with a combination of buckwheat and wholemeal flours. They are perfect for breakfast and brunch, and even for lunch or dinner. This recipe is a double quantity—enjoy a serve for two when freshly cooked and freeze the remaining hotcakes for later.

Corncakes

Preparation time: 10 minutes
Cooking time: 15 minutes
Storage time: Freeze for up to 2 weeks
Makes: 8 hotcakes (4 serves)

¼ cup (45 g/1½ oz) buckwheat flour
½ teaspoon baking powder
½ teaspoon bicarbonate of soda (baking soda)
½ cup (75 g/2½ oz) wholemeal plain flour
½ teaspoon brown sugar
1 (50 g/1¾ oz) egg
1 cup (250 ml/9 fl oz) buttermilk
1 cup (185 g/6½ oz) drained canned sweet corn kernels
¼ cup (50 g/1¾ oz) drained canned lentils
3 teaspoons chopped chives
Oil spray

Sift the buckwheat flour, baking powder and bicarbonate of soda into a mixing bowl. Stir in the wholemeal flour and sugar. Beat the egg, mix with the buttermilk and blend into the flour mixture until smooth. Stir in the corn, lentils and chives. Set aside while preparing the salsa.

Heat a large non-stick frying pan over a medium heat and coat lightly with olive oil spray. Place about two tablespoons of mixture in the pan for each corncake and cook until bubbles appear on the top, about 2–3 minutes (cook 2–3 at a time). Turn the corncakes with a spatula and cook until lightly browned, about 1–2 minutes. Keep warm and continue cooking with the remaining mixture.

Serve two corncakes per person, spread with avocado, topped with salsa (recipe and picture follow).

Nutrition per serve (2 corncakes with salsa)	
Energy kJ (cals)	1295 (309)
Protein	12 g
Total fat	12.7 g
Saturated fat	3.2 g
Fibre	5.2 g
Carbohydrate	37 g
Cholesterol	47 mg
Sodium	433 mg

Red Capsicum (Pepper) Salsa and Avocado

This recipe to serve two with the Buckwheat, Lentil and Chive Corncakes would also be perfect served over poached chicken breast, grilled fish or lean lamb cutlets. It could be stirred through cooked pasta with tuna and the avocado sliced on top.

Preparation time: 5 minutes
Storage time: Refrigerate up to 1 day
Serves: 2

½ cup (80 g/2¾ oz) finely diced red capsicum (pepper)
1 tablespoon drained canned lentils
2 teaspoons chopped chives
1 teaspoon white wine vinegar
½ teaspoon brown sugar
⅓ cup (75 g/2½ oz) mashed avocado
Freshly ground black pepper

Place capsicum, lentils, chives, vinegar and sugar in a bowl and mix to combine. Set aside to allow the flavours to develop. If you make it in advance it will keep for a day in the refrigerator in a covered container. Spread avocado on corncakes, top with salsa and a few grinds of pepper or to taste.

Nutrition per serve	
Energy kJ (cals)	398 (95)
Protein	1.7 g
Total fat	8.6 g
Saturated fat	1.8 g
Fibre	1.2 g
Carbohydrate	3 g
Cholesterol	0 mg
Sodium	16 mg

Banana and Walnut Bread
Low kilojoule, low sodium, medium GI

Preparation time: 15 minutes
Cooking time: 1½ hours
Storage time: Up to 1 week in the refrigerator
Makes: 14 slices

½ cup (60 g/2¼ oz) walnut pieces
1 cup (270 g/10 oz) mashed very ripe
  bananas (3)
2 x 50 g/1¾ oz eggs, lightly beaten
¼ cup (60 ml/2 fl oz) buttermilk
½ cup (125 g/4½ oz) melted and cooled
  plant sterol spread
¼ teaspoon vanilla extract
¾ cup (90 g/3 oz) extra walnut pieces
½ cup (90 g/3 oz) brown sugar
¾ cup (90 g /3 oz) plain flour
¾ cup (110 g/3¾ oz) wholemeal plain flour
2 teaspoons baking powder
½ teaspoon bicarbonate of soda (baking
  soda)

Preheat oven to cool 150°C (300°F/Gas Mark 2) and grease a 21 cm x 9 cm x 6.5 cm (8¼ x 3½ x 2½ inch) deep loaf tin.

Spread walnuts on a baking tray and bake for 6–8 minutes or until lightly golden. Cool.

Combine the bananas, eggs, buttermilk, spread and vanilla together and stir until well mixed.

Place the extra walnuts in the bowl of a food processor and process until they are fine, 20–30 seconds. Add the sugar, plain and wholemeal flours, baking powder and bicarbonate of soda. Process until the ingredients are combined for 30–40 seconds. With the motor running, pour the banana mixture through the funnel of the food processor and process for 30 seconds or until the mixture is well combined. Stir in the toasted walnuts.

Place the mixture into the prepared tin and bake for 1½ hours or until a skewer inserted in the centre comes out clean. Cool in the tin before transferring to a wire rack.

Nutrition note: Stoneground wholemeal flour has a slightly lower GI than regular flour.

Nutrition per serve (1 slice)	
Energy kJ (cals)	985 (236)
Protein	4.8 g
Total fat	15.4 g
Saturated fat	2 g
Fibre	2.3 g
Carbohydrate	20 g
Cholesterol	27 g
Sodium	134 mg

Creamy Yoghurt Rice with Mandarin, Apple and Strawberries
High fibre, low–medium GI

This is an excellent snack to make with leftover cooked brown rice. The creamy yoghurt rice could be made a day ahead and refrigerated and would make a quick dessert. Serve with any fruits in season, canned or stewed fruits. It's high in fibre and very filling—ideal for larger appetites.

Nutrition note: Using basmati, doongara or koshikari rice will lower the GI of this recipe, as will using yellowbox honey or pure maple syrup instead of regular honey.

Preparation time: 10 minutes
Serves: 2

⅔ cup (150 g/5½ oz) cooked and cooled
 brown rice
2 tablespoons currants
2 tablespoons low fat plain yoghurt
1 teaspoon honey
1 × 125 g/4½ oz mandarin, segmented
1 × 150 g/5½ oz apple, sliced
1 cup (125 g/4½ oz) sliced strawberries
Extra honey

Place the rice, currants, yoghurt and honey in a bowl and mix to combine.

Divide the mixture between two 125 ml (4 fl oz) plastic containers and press down firmly. Turn out onto serving plates with the fruit and drizzle with honey if desired.

Nutrition per serve	
Energy kJ (cals)	1017 (243)
Protein	6 g
Total fat	1.1 g
Saturated fat	0.2 g
Fibre	6 g
Carbohydrate	52 g
Cholesterol	1 mg
Sodium	110 mg

Honey Seed and Nut Slice
Low sodium, low GI

Jam packed full of healthy oats, nuts and seeds, cut this slice into bars or squares. It makes a great snack to enjoy with an apple or a bunch of grapes. High in fibre and heart-healthy oils, this is a sweet treat that's good for you.

Preparation time: 10 minutes
Cooking time: 10–15 minutes
Makes: 10 pieces
Serving size: 1 piece

2 tablespoons plant sterol spread
1 tablespoon brown sugar
¼ cup (80 g/3¾ oz) honey
1½ cups (150 g/5½ oz) traditional wholegrain rolled oats
½ cup (60 g/2¼ oz) walnut pieces, chopped
½ cup (70 g/2½ oz) sunflower kernels
¼ cup (30 g/1 oz) ground almonds (almond meal)
¼ cup (45 g/1½ oz) sesame seeds
1 tablespoon (20 g/¾ oz) linseeds

Preheat oven to moderately cool 170°C (325°F/Gas Mark 3) and grease and line a 21 × 9 × 6.5 cm (8¼ × 3½ × 2½ inch) deep loaf tin.

Melt the plant sterol spread, sugar and honey over a low heat, stir until the sugar dissolves. Continue to simmer very gently for 5 minutes.

Mix together the oats, walnuts, sunflower kernels, ground almonds, sesame seeds and linseeds in a large bowl.

Pour the melted mixture into the dry ingredients and mix until well combined. Press mixture very firmly into the prepared tin and bake for 10–15 minutes until light golden brown. If browning too quickly around the edges, cover the edges with foil. Cool completely in the tin.

When cold cut with a serrated knife into bars or squares and store in an airtight container.

Nutrition per serve	
Energy kJ (cals)	822 (196)
Protein	4 g
Total fat	12 g
Saturated fat	1.4 g
Fibre	2 g
Carbohydrate	17 g
Cholesterol	0 mg
Sodium	17 mg

Pistachio, Oat and Almond Biscuits
Low sodium, low GI

This recipe has been adapted from an almond macaroon biscuit. Oats have been added to increase the fibre. The mixture is rolled in pistachios and almonds before baking making them look as delicious as they taste. Enjoy with morning or afternoon coffee or tea. Low in salt, and with the heart-friendly goodness of nuts.

Preparation time: 10 minutes
Refrigeration Time: 1 hour
Cooking time: 20 minutes
Storage time: Store in an airtight container 5 days.
Makes: 20

3 teaspoons plant sterol spread
1 teaspoon honey
1 cup (100 g/3½ oz) flaked almonds
¼ cup (30 g/1 oz) traditional wholegrain
 rolled oats
½ cup (110 g/3½ oz) caster sugar
1 egg white
¼ cup (30 g/1 oz) extra flaked almonds
⅓ cup (45 g/1½ oz) pistachio kernels
Sifted icing sugar for serving, optional

Preheat oven to cool 150°C (300°F/Gas Mark 2) and line a baking tray with baking paper.

Place the plant sterol spread and honey in a microwave safe bowl and melt on 20 per cent power for 30–40 seconds.

Place the almonds, rolled oats and caster sugar in the bowl of a food processor and process for 30 seconds or until fine. With the motor running, pour the egg white and honey mixture through the funnel of the food processor and process for 40 seconds or until the mixture forms a smooth paste. Transfer mixture to a small bowl, cover and refrigerate for 1 hour.

Roughly chop the extra almond flakes and pistachios and mix well to combine.

Shape the biscuit mixture into small balls and roll in the combined almonds and pistachios pressing the nuts firmly into the mixture. Place on the baking tray and press each biscuit gently with a fork and bake for 20 minutes or until the biscuits are lightly browned. Cool on the baking tray before serving sprinkled lightly with icing sugar.

Nutrition per serve (2 biscuits)	
Energy kJ (cals)	707 (161)
Protein	4 g
Total fat	10.6 g
Saturated fat	1.0 g
Fibre	2 g
Carbohydrate	15 g
Cholesterol	0 mg
Sodium	11 mg

Blueberry, Bran and LSA muffins

These mini muffins are delicious served warm when freshly baked or reheat well after refrigerating or freezing. A light sprinkling of icing sugar is optional. These yummy baked treats have the cholesterol-lowering benefits of a plant sterol spread and oat bran as well as the goodness of wholegrains, nuts and seeds. Enjoy with a glass of low fat milk or skim milk café latte.

Preparation time: 10 minutes
Cooking time: 15–20 minutes
Makes: 24 mini-muffins
Serving size: 2 mini-muffins

2 tablespoons plant sterol spread, melted
¾ teaspoon vanilla extract
1 (50 g/1¾ oz) egg, beaten
¾ cup (200ml /7 oz) reduced-fat milk
¾ cup (110 g/3¾ oz) stoneground wholemeal self-raising flour
¼ teaspoon baking powder
¼ cup (30 g/1 oz) Soy and LSA mix (Soy, Linseed, Sunflower and Almond Blend)
1 tablespoon brown sugar
1 tablespoon oat bran
½ cup (75g/2½ oz) blueberries

Topping
2 tablespoons plain stoneground wholemeal flour
1½ tablespoons plant sterol spread
1 tablespoon brown sugar
¼ cup (30g/1 oz) Soy, LSA mix

Preheat oven to moderately hot 200°C (400°F/Gas Mark 6) and grease 2 x 12 cup (30 ml/1 fl oz capacity) muffin trays.

Mix together the plant sterol spread, vanilla, egg and milk.

In a separate bowl, mix together the flour, baking powder, Soy LSA, sugar and bran. Add the wet ingredients to the dry ingredients and stir only until just combined. Fold the blueberries into the mixture.

To make the topping, mix all the ingredients together in a bowl.

Spoon the muffin mixture into the prepared tins and spread a little topping on each muffin. Bake for 15–20 minutes or until cooked. Cool and refrigerate or freeze.

Nutrition per serve (2 mini muffins)	
Energy kJ (cals)	494 (118)
Protein	4 g
Total fat	6.4 g
Saturated fat	1.2 g
Fibre	2.4 g
Carbohydrate	12 g
Cholesterol	17 mg
Sodium	105 mg

25: Light meals

Beef and Soba Noodle Soup with Asian Greens and Mushrooms
Low kilojoule, high fibre, low GI

A complete meal in a bowl. The aromatic ginger, garlic and hoi sin sauce complement the beef, noodles and leafy green vegetables and with the intensity of the mushrooms combine to make a very heart healthy soup. Beef stocks vary in sodium content, so check the label to ensure you buy the lowest—less than 300mg/100 ml is ideal.

Preparation time: 10 minutes
Cooking time: 25 minutes
Serves: 2

90 g (3 oz) soba noodles
¾ cup (185 ml/6 fl oz) salt-reduced beef stock
2 cups (500 ml/17 fl oz) water
2 cloves garlic, chopped
3 teaspoons finely grated ginger
1 cup (125 g/4½ oz) sliced carrot
2 cups (125 g/4½ oz) sliced mushrooms
1 cup (80 g /2¾ oz) thinly sliced Chinese chard (baby bok choy) stems
1 cup (60 g/2¼ oz) thinly sliced Chinese chard (baby bok choy) leaves
100 g/3½ oz thinly sliced lean beef (eye fillet)
3 teaspoons hoi sin sauce
½ teaspoon sesame oil

Bring 1 litre (1¾ pints) of water to the boil in a large pot. Add the noodles and rapidly boil for 4 minutes. Drain, rinse thoroughly in cold water and drain again.

Place stock, water, garlic and ginger in a large pot over a medium heat, cover and bring to the boil. Reduce the heat and cook for 10 minutes.

Add the carrot, mushrooms and Chinese chard stems and cook, covered, for a further 10 minutes.

Stir in the Chinese chard leaves, beef and hoi sin sauce and cook until the leaves are just wilted and the beef is cooked, 2–3 minutes. Stir in sesame oil

Divide the noodles between two serving bowls, pour over the hot soup.

Nutrition per serve	
Energy kJ (cals)	1213 (289)
Protein	20 g
Total fat	5 g
Saturated fat	1.2 g
Fibre	8.4 g
Carbohydrate	40 g
Cholesterol	32 mg
Sodium	420 mg

Tuna and Cracked Wheat Salad
Good source omega-3, high fibre, low GI

This recipe is a variation of tabouli, the flavours of the garlic, pepper sauce and herbs can be varied to suit your taste buds. It is a very portable salad and great to take to work for lunch, ideal for picnics or outdoor activities.

Preparation time: 20 minutes
Serves: 2

½ cup (90g/3 oz)cracked wheat
(bulgar/burghul)
185g (6½ oz) can tuna in oil (e.g.
sunflower/canola/olive oil)
1–2 cloves garlic, crushed
Tabasco (pepper sauce) to taste
2 x 80 g/2¾ oz tomatoes, chopped
1 cup (125 g/4½ oz) diced red onion
1 cup (150g/5½ oz) chopped yellow capsicum (pepper)
¼ cup chopped flat leaf parsley
¼ cup torn basil leaves
Lemon wedges for serving

Place cracked wheat in a bowl and cover with boiling water. Allow to stand 15 minutes or until soft. Drain well.

Drain the tuna, reserving 1 tablespoon of oil. Add the garlic and Tabasco to the reserved oil and mix well.

Combine the tomatoes, onion, capsicum, parsley and drained cracked wheat in a large bowl. Stir in the oil.

Divide salad between two serving bowls, top with the tuna and basil and a lemon wedge.

Nutrition per serve	
Energy kJ (cals)	1718 (411)
Protein	31 g
Total fat	13.8 g
Saturated fat	2.2 g
Fibre	10.9 g
Carbohydrate	35 g
Cholesterol	37 mg
Sodium	443 mg

Fish, Tomato, Saffron and White Bean Soup
Low kilojoule, good source omega-3,
high fibre, low GI

Saffron adds an authentic flavour and rich colour to this Mediterranean influenced soup that could also be made with green peeled prawns or a marinara mix. If you have time you could use fresh tomatoes with the skins and seeds removed.

Preparation time: 10 minutes
Cooking time: 15 minutes
Serves: 2

1 tablespoon olive oil
1 clove garlic, finely chopped
½ cup (60g/2¼ oz) diced white onion
½ cup (60g/2¼ oz) diced carrot
Pinch saffron threads, dissolved in 2 table-spoons boiling water
1 cup (200 g/7 oz) canned whole peeled tomatoes in juice (no added salt)
½ cup (125 ml/4 fl oz) water
½ cup (75g/2½ oz) drained and rinsed canned white beans (butter beans/fagioli)
150 g/5½ oz cubed boneless white fish
1 tablespoon chopped parsley
2 small warm mixed grain rolls or lite wholemeal pita breads

Heat the oil in a saucepan over a medium heat.

Add the garlic, onion and carrot and stir until the onion is soft, 2–3 minutes.

Stir in the dissolved saffron threads and water, tomatoes and water. Stir to break up the tomatoes while bringing to the boil, 1–2 minutes.

Stir in the beans, reduce heat, cover and cook for 5 minutes, stirring occasionally.

Add the fish and stir occasionally for 2–3 minutes or until the fish is cooked.

Stir in the parsley and serve with the rolls.

Nutrition note: Try low sodium wholemeal pita rolls with only 200 mg sodium per 100 g.

Nutrition per serve	
Energy kJ (cals)	1501 (357)
Protein	25 g
Total fat	12 g
Saturated fat	2 g
Fibre	8.5 g
Carbohydrate	36 g
Cholesterol	44 mg
Sodium	345 mg

Sardine, Capers, Mint, Lemon, Rocket (Arugula), on Rye with Tomatoes
Excellent source omega-3, high fibre, low–medium GI

Mint was the inspiration for this recipe as it is one of the most popular of all herbs, tastes wonderful and is often growing in the garden. Combining mint with the sharpness of lemon, the subtle saltiness of the sardines and capers delivers a refreshing taste sensation. Look for wholegrain breads less than 400mg sodium per 100 g.

Preparation time: 10 minutes
Serves: 2

  4 slices wholegrain rye bread
  2 tablespoons light plant sterol spread
  2 x 110 g/3¾ oz cans sardines in springwater, drained
  ¼–½ lemon, rind, pith and seeds removed and finely diced
  3 teaspoons (15 g/½ oz) drained baby capers in wine vinegar
  ¼ cup torn mint leaves
  ¼ cup trimmed rocket (arugula)
  ⅔ cup (100 g/3½ oz) halved cherry tomatoes

Spread the bread with the spread.

Place the sardines in a bowl and lightly mash with a fork, add the lemon, capers and mint and mix to combine.

Place the bread on two serving plates, pile the sardine mixture onto each piece of bread and top with rocket.

Scatter the tomatoes over or on the side of the sandwiches and serve.

Nutrition note: We used rye bread with other mixed grains and seeds with 360 mg/100 g sodium.

Cook's tip: Two 110 g/3¾ oz cans of sardines in springwater yield a drained mass of 150 g/5½ oz, that is the recommended serving size for two serves.

Nutrition per serve	
Energy kJ (cals)	1760 (420)
Protein	27 g
Total fat	19.8 g
Saturated fat	4 g
Fibre	3.6 g
Carbohydrate	28 g
Cholesterol	70 mg
Sodium	485 mg

Sweet Potato and Kidney Bean Patties with Salad and Cottage Cheese
Low kilijoule, low sodium, high fibre, low–medium GI

Preparation time: 15 minutes
Cooking time: 20 minutes
Serves: 2

Patties

250 g (9 oz) sweet potato, peeled and cut into large chunks
1 clove garlic, crushed
1 teaspoon garam masala
1 small/½ cup (60 g/2¼ oz) diced zucchini
½ cup (60 g/2¼ oz) diced red onion
¼ cup (50g/1¾ oz) drained and rinsed canned red kidney beans
1 tablespoon wholemeal plain flour
1 tablespoon canola oil
2 tablespoons low fat cottage cheese
1 x 25 g (1 oz) piece whole wheat flat bread (lavash)

Salad

1 cup torn mesclun
½ cup (75 g/2½ oz) halved cherry tomatoes
¼ cup (50 g/1¾ oz) drained and rinsed canned red kidney beans
½ cup (60 g/2¼ oz) diced zucchini
2 teaspoons balsamic vinegar

To make the patties: Place the sweet potato in a saucepan and cover with cold water. Cover, bring to the boil on high heat, reduce heat and cook, covered, 5 minutes or until the potato is tender. Drain well, cool and mash.

Add the garlic, garam masala, zucchini, onion and kidney beans to the mashed potato and mix well. Shape into four even patties. (The mixture should be easy to handle, if it is too soft, mix in a little wholemeal flour.)

Place the flour into a plastic bag add the patties one at a time and shake until coated with flour.

Heat the oil in a large non-stick frying pan over a medium heat and cook the patties until golden on each side and cooked through, 10–12 minutes.

Serve the patties drizzled with cottage cheese and with the salad on the side.

To make the salad: Combine the mesclun, tomatoes, kidney beans, zucchini and vinegar.

Cut the flat bread into 2.5 cm/1 inch squares and stir through the salad just before serving.

Nutrition per serve	
Energy kJ (cals)	1280 (305)
Protein	12 g
Total fat	10.4 g
Saturated fat	2 g
Fibre	9 g
Carbohydrate	41 g
Cholesterol	3 mg
Sodium	297 mg

Honey and Five Spice Pork Noodles
Medium GI

Have all the ingredients prepared before starting to cook this recipe. It is delicious served hot or is suitable to be refrigerated and enjoyed the following day. If you like more heat and herb, serve sliced chilli, Thai basil and a wedge of lime on the side.

Preparation time: 15 minutes
Cooking time: 10 minutes
Serves: 2

60 g/2 oz vermicelli rice noodles, dry
3 teaspoons hoi sin sauce
1 teaspoon salt-reduced soy sauce
1½ tablespoons honey
1½ teaspoons rice wine vinegar
½ teaspoon Chinese five spice powder
1 tablespoon peanut oil
100 g/3½ oz sliced pork fillet
1 cup (150 g/5½ oz) diced red capsicum
¾ cup (150 g/5½ oz) diced celery
1 cup (60 g/2¼ oz) sliced spring onions
(shallots)

Bring 1 litre (1¾ pints) of water to the boil in a large pot. Add the noodles and cook for 3–5 minutes. Drain and rinse under cold water.

Mix together the hoi sin sauce, soy, honey, vinegar and five spice.

Heat the oil in a wok over a high heat and cook the pork until golden, 3–4 minutes. Add the capsicum, celery and spring onions and stir-fry for 2–3 minutes. Add the hoi sin sauce mixture and stir for 1–2 minutes.

Stir in the drained noodles and cook until hot.

Cook's tip: To cook the pork until golden brown, have the pan and oil really hot before adding the pork and leave it to cook for about a minute or two before turning or stirring. If the pork has browned well it will be easy to move around the pan.

Nutrition per serve	
Energy kJ (cals)	1963 (470)
Protein	18 g
Total fat	11.7 g
Saturated fat	2.1 g
Fibre	4.3 g
Carbohydrate	73 g
Cholesterol	48 mg
Sodium	377 mg

Lamb, Minted Pea and Rosemary Couscous
Low sodium, high fibre, low GI

Couscous is traditionally served as an accompaniment to tagines, however, it is a very versatile ingredient and makes a great grain base for salads and complete meals. This recipe can be served hot or at room temperature.

Preparation time: 15 minutes
Cooking time: 15 minutes
Serves: 2

Couscous
2 teaspoons olive oil
1 medium/1 cup (125 g/4½ oz) sliced onion
1 clove garlic, crushed
100 g/3½ oz thinly sliced lamb loin eye
½ cup (75 g/2½ oz) frozen peas
¼ cup (60 ml/2 fl oz) salt-reduced vegetable stock
¼ cup (60 ml/2 fl oz) water
½ cup (100 g/3½ oz) couscous
1 tablespoon shredded mint leaves
½ cup (75 g/2½ oz) quartered grape tomatoes
⅓ cup (60 g/2¼ oz) canned drained chickpeas

Dressing
1 teaspoon olive oil
1 teaspoon white wine vinegar
½ teaspoon brown sugar
½ teaspoon finely chopped rosemary

To make the couscous: Heat oil in a non-stick frying pan over a medium heat. Add the onion and garlic and cook until golden, 3–4 minutes.

Add the lamb and stir for 2–3 minutes.

Add peas and stir occasionally until the peas are cooked, 2–3 minutes.

Meanwhile, bring the stock and water to the boil and slowly pour in the couscous, remove from the heat, cover and let stand for 2–3 minutes before stirring with a fork to separate the grains.

Place the couscous in a large bowl, stir in the lamb mixture, mint, tomatoes, chickpeas and dressing.

Dressing: Combine the oil, vinegar, sugar and rosemary and stir well.

Nutrition per serve	
Energy kJ (cals)	1607 (384)
Protein	22 g
Total fat	9.8 g
Saturated fat	1.9 g
Fibre	6 g
Carbohydrate	51 g
Cholesterol	33 mg
Sodium	225 mg

Smoked Paprika Chicken and Corn Frittata with Cos and Capsicum Salad
Low kiojoule, low sodium, low–medium GI

Preparation time: 15 minutes
Cooking time: 10 minutes
Baking time: 25 minutes
Serves: 2

3 teaspoons canola oil
100 g/3½ oz sliced chicken breast fillet
1 cup (80 g/2¾ oz) sliced leek (white part only)
1 teaspoon sweet smoked paprika
2 x 50 g/1¾ oz eggs (omega-3 enriched)
¼ cup (75 g/2½ oz) creamed corn
1 teaspoon wholemeal plain flour
2 teaspoons chopped chives
2 tablespoons (50 g/1¾ oz) creamed corn, extra

Salad
3 cups torn baby cos lettuce
1 cup (100 g/3½ oz) finely sliced red, capsicum
3 teaspoons vinaigrette dressing

Preheat oven to moderate 180°C (350°F/Gas Mark 4) and grease and base line, with baking paper, 2 x 10cm (4 inch) diameter ovenproof dishes.

Heat oil in a non-stick frying pan over a high heat and brown the chicken, 2–3 minutes. Reduce heat and stir in the leek and cook for 3–4 minutes or until the chicken is cooked and the leek is soft. Stir in the paprika and cook for a further 1 minute. Divide mixture between the two prepared dishes.

Beat the eggs lightly and mix in the corn, flour and chives and pour evenly over the chicken.

Bake for 20–25 minutes or until golden and set. Cool for a few minutes and then turn out of the dishes, remove the baking paper and place on warmed serving plates.

Serve with the extra creamed corn and salad.

Nutrition note: This is a good example of a recipe that is higher in fat and cholesterol but still low in saturated fat. If you're watching your weight, kilojoules are the most important thing to limit and the kilojoules in this recipe are low.

Nutrition per serve	
Energy kJ (cals)	1390 (332)
Protein	19 g
Total fat	21.8 g
Saturated fat	3.9 g
Fibre	4.7 g
Carbohydrate	16 g
Cholesterol	190 mg
Sodium	297 mg

Tofu, Spinach and Satay Rice
High fibre, low–medium GI

This recipe uses a commercial satay sauce that adds great flavour—check the nutrition label when purchasing the sauce and choose the lowest in sodium and saturated fat. Try substituting the rice with barley or chickpeas for variety.

Preparation time: 10 minutes
Cooking time: 35 minutes
Serves: 2

⅓ cup (70 g/2½ oz) brown rice
⅔ cup (170 ml/5½ fl oz) water
2 tablespoons raw peanuts
3 teaspoons peanut oil
1½ cups (125 g/4½ oz) brown onion wedges
1 cup (125 g/4½ oz) sliced carrot
2 cups tightly packed torn silverbeet or
  spinach leaves
¼ cup (60 ml/2¼ fl oz) satay simmer sauce*
300 g/10½ oz well-drained and cubed soft
  silken tofu
1 long (30 g/1 oz) medium heat red chilli,
  sliced

Place the rice and water in a saucepan over a medium heat and bring to the boil, stir occasionally. Reduce heat, cover and simmer for 25–30 minutes. Remove from the heat and stand, covered, for 5-10 minutes before using. Heat a non-stick frying pan over a medium/low heat and dry roast the peanuts for 1–2 minutes and set aside.

Heat the oil in the same pan and cook the onions until golden, 2–3 minutes. Add the carrot and cook for 1–2 minutes. Add the silverbeet and cook until the leaves are just wilted, 1–2 minutes.

Stir the satay sauce and vegetables through the rice and mix well.

Divide the rice between two bowls and top with the tofu, peanuts and chilli.

*Cook's tip: A simmer sauce is used as a recipe ingredient, typically in stir-fries, and is lower in sodium and saturated fat than a condiment (e.g. ketchup) style sauce. You could also use a smaller quantity (2–3 teaspoons) of a more concentrated satay recipe base (paste).

Nutrition note: Using brown basmati rice will lower the GI.

Nutrition per serve	
Energy kJ (cals)	1673 (400)
Protein	19.9 g
Total fat	17.8 g
Saturated fat	3.6 g
Fibre	6.6 g
Carbohydrate	41 g
Cholesterol	1.6 mg
Sodium	396 mg

Chicken, Dill, Chive, Cheese and Cashew Wrap with Tomato, Lettuce and Asparagus

Low sodium, high fibre

Preparation time: 10 minutes
Cooking time: 10 minutes
Serves: 2

The delicious herb and cashew mixture in this recipe is made with heart-healthy oils and is full of flavour. It makes a great spread on any meat, salmon or tuna sandwich and would be perfect dolloped on lean barbecued meats or seafood.

1 tablespoon chopped dill
1 tablespoon chopped chives
2 tablespoons (20 g /¾ oz) natural cashew kernels, chopped
1 tablespoon (7g /¼ oz) very finely grated parmesan cheese
3 teaspoons extra virgin olive oil
1 x 250 g/9 oz bunch green asparagus, trimmed
Canola oil cooking spray
100 g /3½ oz chicken breast fillet
2 cups baby lettuce leaves (mesclun)
2 x 75 g/2½ oz tomatoes, quartered
2 wholemeal flat breads (eg flat bread or lavash)
2 tablespoons (40 g /1½ oz) extra light cream cheese (5% fat)

Place the dill, chives, cashews, parmesan and olive oil in a small bowl and mix well. Set aside to allow the flavours to develop.

Steam or microwave the asparagus. Allow to cool.

Heat a non-stick pan over a medium heat and spray with oil and cook the chicken, 6–8 minutes or until cooked, turning once. Wrap in foil to rest and cool.

Place the salad leaves, tomatoes, asparagus and half the dill, chive, cashew and parmesan mixture in a bowl and mix well.

Slice the chicken thinly. Spread the breads with cream cheese.

Spread the remaining dill, chive, cashew and parmesan mixture over half of each bread with the chicken and roll up tightly.

Cut the wraps into three or four pieces. Serve the wraps with the salad.

Nutrition per serve	
Energy kJ (cals)	1661 (395)
Protein	26 g
Total fat	18.8 g
Saturated fat	4.3 g
Fibre	6.4 g
Carbohydrate	30 g
Cholesterol	50 mg
Sodium	269 mg

26: Mains

Beef, Creamy Mushroom and Broccolini Penne with a Mixed Leaf Salad

Low sodium, high fibre, low GI

Preparation time: 15 minutes
Cooking time: 20 minutes
Serves: 2

1½ cups (125 g/4½ oz) wholemeal penne
1 tablespoon sunflower oil
200 g/7 oz piece lean beef (eye fillet)
1 cup (125 g/4½ oz) diced onion
1 clove garlic, crushed
¾ cup (125 g/4 oz) diced carrot
2 x 90 g/3 oz flat mushrooms, diced
250 g/9 oz bunch broccolini or broccoli,
  trimmed, stems diced and florets reserved
1 cup (250 ml/9 fl oz) light evaporated milk
  (1.5 % fat)
2 teaspoons corn flour, blended with
  2 teaspoons water

Mixed leaf salad

2 cups torn mixed salad leaves
2 x 40 g(1½ oz) tomatoes cut into quarters
3 teaspoons herb vinaigrette (see recipe
  page 41)

Bring 1¼ litres (2½ pints) of water to the boil in a large pot. Add the penne and continue to boil for approximately 9–11 minutes or until when tasted the penne is cooked as liked. Drain.

Heat the oil in a non-stick frying pan over a medium heat. Add the beef to the pan and cook, 8–10 minutes, turning once, or until cooked as liked. Wrap in foil and rest in a warm place while preparing the sauce and vegetables—this makes it easier to slice.

Add the onion and garlic to the pan and cook, stirring occasionally, until soft, 3–4 minutes. Add the carrot, mushrooms and broccolini stems and cook, stirring occasionally, until soft, 3–4 minutes.

Stir in the evaporated milk and bring to the boil. Add the blended corn flour and stir until thickens. Stir in the drained pasta and reheat.

Meanwhile, steam or microwave the broccolini florets 2–3 minutes and slice the beef finely across the grain. To make the salad, combine the leaves and tomato in a bowl and toss with the herb vinaigrette.

Serve pasta topped with beef slices, any meat juices, broccolini and the salad.

Nutrition per serve	
Energy kJ (cals)	2746 (656)
Protein	50 g
Total fat	21.5
Saturated fat	4.4 g
Fibre	17 g
Carbohydrate	65 g
Cholesterol	74 mg
Sodium	261 mg

Oregano Lamb, Risoni and Borlotti Beans with Fennel, Olive and Zucchini Salad

Low sodium, high fibre, low GI

Preparation time: 15 minutes
Cooking time: 40 minutes
Serves: 2

1 tablespoon olive oil
1 clove garlic, crushed
1 cup (125 g/4½ oz) sliced brown onion
1½ teaspoons dried oregano
¾ teaspoon sweet smoked paprika
¾ teaspoon cumin
200 g/7 oz lean lamb (boneless leg chops)
1 cup (250 ml/9 fl oz) water
400 g/14 oz can whole peeled tomatoes (no added salt)
1 tablespoon lemon juice
1 teaspoon sugar
½ cup (100 g/3½ oz) risoni
1 cup (100 g/3½ oz) drained canned borlotti beans
Chopped flat leaf parsley

Salad

1 medium/1 cup (90 g/3 oz) finely sliced fennel bulb
2 tablespoons (30 g/1 oz) halved, pitted kalamata olives
1 cup (125 g/4½ oz) diced yellow zucchini (courgettes)
1 cup (125 g/4½ oz) diced green zucchini (courgettes)
1½ tablespoons orange juice

Heat the oil in a large saucepan over a medium heat. Add the garlic and onion and stir for 1–2 minutes until soft and transparent. Stir in the oregano, paprika and cumin and cook for 1 minute. Add the lamb and brown, stirring, for 2–3 minutes.

Add the water, tomatoes, lemon juice and sugar and bring to the boil. Reduce the heat, cover and simmer gently for 20 minutes or until the lamb is tender. Stir in the risoni and cook, stirring occasionally for 8 minutes or until the risoni is cooked and the juices are almost absorbed. Add a little water if required. Stir in the borlotti beans and heat through.

To make the salad: Combine the fennel, olives and zucchini in a bowl and toss with the orange juice.

Serve the lamb sprinkled with parsley and salad.

Nutrition per serve	
Energy kJ (cals)	2394 (572)
Protein	37 g
Total fat	17.5 g
Saturated fat	4.5 g
Fibre	10 g
Carbohydrate	68 g
Cholesterol	68 mg
Sodium	232 mg

Warm Beef Salad with Lime, Sweet Chilli and Herb Dressing

High fibre, low GI

Preparation time: 10 minutes
Cooking time: 12 minutes
Resting Time: 5–10 minutes
Serves: 2

Beef salad

2 teaspoons peanut oil
1 tablespoon raw peanuts
200 g/7 oz piece lean beef (eye fillet)
2 cups torn oak lettuce leaves
1¼ large (180 g/6½ oz) sliced red capsicum
1 cup (150 g/5½ oz) sliced cucumber
1 cup (125 g/4½ oz) sliced red onion
1½ cups (125 g/4½ oz) mixed sprouts
2 small multigrain bread rolls

Lime, Sweet Chilli and Herb Dressing

Zest and juice of 1 lime
2 teaspoons white vinegar
1 teaspoon grated ginger
1 tablespoon sweet chilli sauce
½ teaspoon fish sauce
½ teaspoon salt-reduced soy sauce
1 teaspoon palm or brown sugar
2 teaspoons peanut oil
¼ cup tightly packed mint leaves
¼ cup tightly packed coriander leaves

Heat the oil in a non-stick frying pan over a medium heat and cook the peanuts for 1–2 minutes or until golden brown, set aside on paper towel to cool then chop roughly.

Add the beef to the pan and cook, 8–10 minutes, turning once or until cooked as liked. Wrap in foil and rest in a warm place while preparing the salad to allow the meat juices to settle.

To make the dressing, place all the ingredients in a blender and puree until smooth or chop the mint and coriander finely and combine all the ingredients in a screw-top jar and shake well.

Slice the beef across the grain finely.

Combine the lettuce leaves, capsicum, cucumber, onion and sprouts in a large bowl and toss well with the dressing. Top with beef slices, any meat juices and the chopped peanuts and serve with the rolls.

Nutrition per serve	
Energy kJ (cals)	1976 (472)
Protein	33 g
Total fat	18.9 g
Saturated fat	4.4 g
Fibre	9 g
Carbohydrate	41 g
Cholesterol	67 mg
Sodium	555 mg

Barbecued Chermoula Lamb, Pumpkin and Eggplant Burghul with Yoghurt and Coriander
High fibre

Chermoula is a dry, North African spice blend. You can buy it in most large supermarkets or specialities delis.

Preparation time: 20 minutes
Marinating time: 20 minutes
Cooking time: 25 minutes
Serves: 2

200 g/7 oz piece lean lamb (loin eye)
2 teaspoons chermoula spice mix
½ cup (90 g/3 oz) fine burghul (bulgar)
1 cup (250 ml/9 fl oz) boiling water
1 teaspoon chermoula spice, extra
2 cups (300 g/10½ oz) diced butternut
   pumpkin
½ cup (60 g/2¼ oz) sliced green beans
1 tablespoon olive oil
1 cup (125 g/4½ oz) sliced onion
2¼ cups (170 g/6 oz) sliced eggplant
   (aubergine)
oil spray
½ cup (125 g/4½ fl oz) low fat yoghurt
2 tablespoons chopped coriander leaves

Sprinkle the chermoula spice all over the lamb and press into the flesh; cover and refrigerate for 20 minutes.

Meanwhile, place the burghul, boiling water and extra chermoula in a bowl and allow to stand for 15 minutes or until soft.

Place the pumpkin in a small saucepan, just cover with water and cook, covered, until tender, 4–5 minutes, add the beans and cook for a further 1–2 minutes. Drain, reserving ¼ cup (60 ml/2 fl oz) of the cooking liquid.

Heat oil in a non-stick pan over a medium heat and cook the onion for 1–2 minutes. Add the eggplant and stir occasionally, for 5 minutes or until cooked. Stir in the pumpkin, beans, reserved cooking liquid and burghul and cook, stirring, for 1–2 minutes. Keep warm.

Spray a barbecue with olive oil spray and cook the lamb as liked, turning once. Wrap in foil to rest in a warm place for 5 minutes then slice finely across the grain.

Serve burghul topped with lamb, yoghurt and coriander.

Nutrition per serve	
Energy kJ (cals)	2578 (616)
Protein	39 g
Total fat	19 g
Saturated fat	5.2 g
Fibre	16 g
Carbohydrate	71 g
Cholesterol	71 mg
Sodium	543 mg

Herbie's chermoula spice mix

If you want to blend your own chermoula, try Ian Hemphill of Herbie's Spices (www.herbies.com.au) favourite mix. You can also change the proportions and make it more like a salsa with the onion and fresh herbs forming the bulk of the mixture, which you then lightly spice. Simply combine all ingredients and use to dry marinate meat, chicken or a firm fleshed fish like tuna for about 20 minutes before cooking.

½ onion finely chopped
1 teaspoon finely chopped fresh coriander
leaves
2 teaspoons finely chopped fresh parsley
1 clove garlic, crushed
3 teaspoons ground cumin seed
2 teaspoons mild paprika
1 teaspoon turmeric
pinch cayenne
ground black pepper to taste

Makes about ⅓ cup

Barbecued Chicken, Corn Cobs and Potato and Baby Beet Salad
Low sodium, high fibre, medium GI

Preparation time: 15 minutes
Cooking time: 20 minutes
Serves: 2

200 g/7oz chicken breast fillet
2 x 200 g/7 oz corn cobs
3 teaspoons sunflower oil
300 g/10½ oz pink eye or desiree potatoes, scrubbed
⅔ cup (125 g/4½ oz) halved canned baby beets
2 cups baby salad leaves (mesclun)
½ cup (60 g/2¼ oz) sliced golden shallots or onion

Dressing
1 tablespoon white wine vinegar
2 teaspoons honey
½ teaspoon wholegrain mustard
½ teaspoon crushed garlic
2 teaspoons extra virgin olive oil

Slice the chicken breast horizontally through the centre into two even thinner fillets. Trim the corn and cut each cob into three even pieces.

Heat a barbecue or griddle pan over a medium heat and brush the chicken and corn with oil. Place them on the barbecue and cook for 5–8 minutes, turning as required. Remove the chicken when cooked and wrap in foil and rest in a warm place. Cook the corn for a further 8–10 minutes or until cooked.

Meanwhile, cook the potatoes, drain and cool and cut into large chunks. Combine dressing ingredients.

Combine the baby beets, salad leaves, shallots and potatoes in a bowl and toss with half the dressing.

Serve the chicken and corn drizzled with the remaining dressing and any chicken juices with the salad.

Cook's tip: Try roasting fresh beetroot, it's easy and the result is excellent. Trim a bunch of beetroot, wash and dry. Wrap beetroots individually in foil and place in a baking dish. Roast in a preheated moderate oven (180°C/350°F/Gas Mark 4) and roast for about 1 hour.

Nutrition per serve	
Energy kJ (cals)	2449 (585)
Protein	35 g
Total fat	20 g
Saturated fat	3.3 g
Fibre	15 g
Carbohydrate	65 g
Cholesterol	66 mg
Sodium	322 mg

Tandoori Chicken with Yoghurt Sauce and Lettuce, Tomato, Cucumber, Mint and Mango Salad

High fibre, low GI

The availability of tandoori pastes on the market makes it easy to recreate authentic Indian flavours at home. You can choose from mild to hot.

Preparation time: 15 minutes
Marinating Time: 30 minutes or overnight
Cooking time: 15 minutes
Serves: 2

200 g/7 oz chicken breast fillet
2 tablespoons low fat plain yoghurt
1 tablespoon tandoori paste*
3 teaspoons sunflower oil*
2 small wholemeal pita breads
* look for the brand lowest in sodium

Yoghurt sauce
⅓ cup low fat plain yoghurt
1 teaspoon tandoori paste, extra
2 teaspoons finely chopped mint
½ teaspoon crushed garlic
⅓ cup puree mango flesh

Salad
2 cups torn mixed salad leaves
2 × 150 g/5½ oz tomatoes, quartered
1 cup (150 g/5½ oz) sliced cucumber
½ cup torn mint leaves
⅔ cup chopped mango flesh

Slice the chicken breast horizontally through the centre into two even thinner fillets.

To make the marinade, mix the yoghurt and tandoori paste in a bowl until smooth and brush over the chicken pieces coating them thoroughly. Place the chicken on a flat dish, cover and refrigerate for 30 minutes.

Heat the oil in a non-stick pan over a medium/low heat and cook the chicken, 8–10 minutes or until cooked, turning once. Wrap in foil and rest in a warm place. To make the Yoghurt Sauce, mix the yoghurt, tandoori paste, mint, garlic and mango in a small bowl.

To make the salad, toss the lettuce, tomato, cucumber, mint and mango together in a bowl.

Serve the salad topped with chicken and any chicken juices and a dollop of sauce with a round wholemeal pita bread.

Nutrition per serve	
Energy kJ (cals)	2104 (502)
Protein	36 g
Total fat	18 g
Saturated fat	3 g
Fibre	10 g
Carbohydrate	46 g
Cholesterol	69 mg
Sodium	637 mg

Steak with Grilled Capsicums, Mushroom and Dill Roasted Buckwheat

Low sodium, low GI

Preparation time: 15 minutes
Cooking time: 25 minutes
Serves: 2

1 × 200 g/7 oz red capsicum (pepper)
1 × 200 g/7 oz orange or yellow capsicum
2 teaspoons olive oil
2 × 60 g/2¼ oz flat mushrooms, stems trimmed
2 × 100 g/3½ oz lean beef fillet or rump steaks
¼ cup (60 ml/2 fl oz) salt-reduced beef stock
¾ cup 200 ml/7 fl oz water
2 tablespoons (50 g/1¾ oz) tomato paste (no added salt)
½ cup (100 g/3½ oz) roasted or raw buckwheat
1 teaspoon olive oil, extra
2 teaspoons balsamic vinegar
2 tablespoons chopped dill
½ avocado (90 g/3 oz), sliced

Cut each capsicum lengthways into four large slices, remove any white membrane and discard the seeds. To roast the capsicums, heat a grill to medium–high heat and place the capsicums skin side up on the rack of the griller tray and brush lightly with a little of the oil. Grill, without turning, until the skin of the capsicum blackens, about 8–10 minutes. Remove capsicums and place in a freezer bag to sweat for 5–10 minutes.

Place the mushrooms, stem side down, and the steaks on the griller rack and brush lightly with oil. Grill for 3–4 minutes on each side until the mushrooms are cooked and the steak cooked as liked. Wrap the steak in foil and rest in a warm place while preparing the buckwheat and vegetables.

Blend the stock, water and tomato paste in a saucepan and bring to the boil, stir in the buckwheat and reduce heat to low. Simmer for 7–10 minutes, stirring occasionally, until the buckwheat is tender and the liquid is almost absorbed. Add extra liquid if needed.

While the buckwheat is cooking, peel and slice the capsicums and chop the mushrooms. Stir into the cooked buckwheat and allow to heat through. Remove from the heat and gently stir in the extra oil, vinegar and dill.

Slice the steak across the grain finely. Place half the buckwheat mixture on each plate and top with the beef slices and avocado.

Nutrition per serve	
Energy kJ (cals)	2279 (544)
Protein	35 g
Total fat	24 g
Saturated fat	5.6 g
Fibre	6.8 g
Carbohydrate	47 g
Cholesterol	67 mg
Sodium	189 mg

Dill Risotto with Chargrilled Salmon and Asparagus, Baby Carrots and Aioli

Low sodium, excellent source of omega-3, high fibre, low–medium GI

It is worth spending the time to cook this risotta slowly. A risotto made with brown rice does not give the creaminess of a traditional recipe made with Arborio rice but the healthy heart benefits are great.

Preparation time: 10 minutes
Cooking time: 35 minutes
Serves: 2

½ cup (125 ml/4 fl oz) salt-reduced chicken stock
3 cups (750 ml/1 pint 6 fl oz) water
1 tablespoon olive oil
1 cup (125 g/4½ oz) sliced onion
1 clove garlic, crushed
½ cup (100 g/3½ oz) brown rice, rinsed
1 tablespoon chopped dill
2 x 150 g/5½ oz skinless salmon fillets
1 x 250 g/9 oz bunch green asparagus, trimmed
oil spray
8–16 (200 g/7 oz) baby carrots, scrubbed and trimmed
1 tablespoon aioli (see recipe page 48)

Place the stock and water in a saucepan, cover and bring to the boil. Reduce heat and leave to simmer.

Heat the oil in a saucepan over a medium heat; add the onion and garlic and cook, stirring, for 2–3 minutes until the onion is soft. Add the rice and stir until rice grains are coated. Add a cup of stock and stir until the liquid is completely absorbed. Continue cooking the rice, adding only a cup of stock at a time, until the rice is tender, about 25–30 minutes. Add more liquid if required. Stir in the dill.

Meanwhile, heat a griddle pan over a medium heat and spray with the oil. Place the fish on the griddle with the asparagus. Cook the fish for 5–8 minutes, turning once and the asparagus for a further 2–5 minutes if needed, turning as required. Set aside, cover with foil and keep hot.

Steam or microwave the carrots.

Serve the risotto, topped with the fish, a dollop of aioli, carrots and asparagus.

Nutrition note: Using brown basmati rice will lower the GI.

Nutrition per serve	
Energy kJ (cals)	2530 (605)
Protein	38 g
Total fat	28 g
Saturated fat	4.4 g
Fibre	7.9 g
Carbohydrate	50 g
Cholesterol	78 mg
Sodium	330 mg

Pork in Pomegranate and Apple Sauce with Pine nuts and Za'atar and Kidney Bean Couscous Salad

High fibre, low GI

Preparation time: 15 minutes
Cooking time: 35 minutes
Serves: 2

oil spray
3 teaspoons (10 g/⅓ oz) pine nuts
2 x 100 g/3½ oz lean pork loin medallions
1 x 200 g/7 oz green apple, peeled and sliced
½ cup (125 ml/4 fl oz) salt-reduced chicken stock
½ cup (125 ml/4 fl oz) water
2 teaspoons pomegranate concentrated juice
Salad
½ cup (125ml/4 fl oz) water
1½ tablespoons za'atar
½ cup (100 g/3½ oz) instant couscous
1 teaspoon plant sterol spread
1 cup (125 g/4½ oz) finely diced zucchini (courgettes)
½ cup (60 g/2¼ oz) finely diced carrot
½ cup (60 g/2¼ oz) finely sliced red onion
⅔ cup (125 g/4½ oz) drained, rinsed canned kidney beans
1 tablespoon chopped flat leaf parsley

Heat a non-stick frying pan over a medium/high heat and spray with oil. Add the pine nuts and cook, stirring, 1–2 minutes. Set aside. Spray the pan with a little more oil and add the pork. Brown on each side, 2–3 minutes, reduce heat and then cook as liked. Wrap in foil to rest.

Add the apple to the pan and stir for 1–2 minutes, add the stock, water and pomegranate juice. Cover and simmer for 3–5 minutes until the apple is tender. Remove the lid and cook for a further 2–3 minutes. Add any pork juices and keep warm.

To make the couscous: place the water and za'atar in a saucepan over a medium heat, cover and bring the water to the boil. Slowly pour in the couscous, remove from the heat, cover and stand for 2–3 minutes. Stir with a fork to separate the grains and mix in the plant sterol spread. Stir in the zucchini, carrot, onion, kidney beans and parsley.

Slice the pork and serve over the couscous with the apple sauce sprinkled with pine nuts.

Nutrition per serve	
Energy kJ (cals)	2016 (482)
Protein	37 g
Total fat	9.7 g
Saturated fat	1.6 g
Fibre	9 g
Carbohydrate	61 g
Cholesterol	95 mg
Sodium	588 mg

Green Vegetable and Tofu Curry with Kaffir Lime Leaves, Toasted Water Chestnuts, Choy Sum and Amaranth Rice

High fibre

Preparation time: 15 minutes
Cooking time: 40 minutes
Serves: 2

½ cup (100 g/3½ oz) brown medium grain rice

250 ml (1 cup/9 fl oz) water

2 teaspoons peanut oil

1 tablespoon green curry paste (look for the brand lowest in sodium)

1 cup (250 ml/9 fl oz) light coconut milk (6% fat)

2 teaspoons brown sugar

½ teaspoon fish sauce

1 piece (150 g/5½ oz) pumpkin, peeled and diced

1 cup (125 g/4½ oz) sliced carrot

300 g/10½ oz firm tofu, cubed

150 g/5½ oz trimmed choy sum leaves

125 g/4½ oz drained sliced water chestnuts

olive oil spray

½ cup (10 g/⅓ oz) amaranth breakfast cereal

1 kaffir leaf or the zest of 1 lime, finely shredded

Place the rice and water in a saucepan over a medium heat. Bring to the boil, stirring occasionally. Reduce heat, cover and simmer for 25–30 minutes. Remove from the heat and stand, covered, for 5–10 minutes before using.

Heat the oil in a non-stick saucepan over a low heat and cook the curry paste for 1–2 minutes stirring until fragrant.

Stir in the coconut milk, sugar, fish sauce, pumpkin and carrot. Bring to the boil, reduce heat and simmer for 10 minutes or until the vegetables are cooked, stirring occasionally. Stir in the tofu and heat through gently.

Meanwhile, steam the choy sum leaves until just wilted, 2–3 minutes.

Pat the water chestnuts dry on paper towel and heat a non-stick frying pan over a medium heat and spray with oil. Cook the chestnuts, stirring, for 5 minutes or until crisp and brown.

Stir the amaranth through the cooked rice.

Serve the rice topped with the curry, kaffir lime and water chestnut chips, with choy sum.

Nutrition per serve	
Energy kJ (cals)	2653 (634)
Protein	32 g
Total fat	24 g
Saturated fat	6.8 g
Fibre	11 g
Carbohydrate	73 g
Cholesterol	3 mg
Sodium	545 mg

Saucy Chocolate and Almond Puddings with Raspberries
High fibre, low GI

These little puddings have been developed to incorporate a little heart-friendly dark chocolate with the goodness of almonds into a really satisfying treat for the chocolate lover.

Preparation time: 15 minutes
Cooking time: 6 minutes
Standing time: 5
Serves: 2

2 tablespoons (20 g ¾ oz) self-raising wholemeal flour
3 teaspoons ground almonds (almond meal)
1 tablespoon (20 g/¾ oz) caster sugar
1½ teaspoons cocoa powder, sifted
1 teaspoon plant sterol spread
15 g/½ oz good quality dark chocolate, chopped
1½ tablespoons (30 ml/1 fl oz) skim milk
1 teaspoon vanilla extract
Extra plant sterol spread for greasing
1 tablespoon brown sugar
2 teaspoons cocoa powder, extra
⅓ cup (80 ml/2½ oz) boiling water
1 cup (150 g/5½ oz) fresh raspberries

Place the flour, almonds, sugar and cocoa powder into a bowl and mix to combine.

Place the spread and chocolate into a microwave safe bowl and microwave on medium 70% power for 20–30 seconds. Mix to combine. Stir in the dry ingredients, milk and vanilla and mix well.

Rub 2 x 200 ml/7 oz microwave safe dishes or cups with the extra spread and spoon the mixture evenly into the dishes.

Sift together the sugar and extra cocoa and sprinkle evenly over each pudding. Carefully pour half the boiling water over each pudding and cover loosely with microwave safe plastic wrap.

Place dishes on baking paper and microwave on defrost (10% power) for 3–5 minutes. The puddings will be cooked when the cake has risen to the top and has set. Stand puddings for about 5 minutes before serving with raspberries.

Cook's tip: Puddings can be baked in a moderate oven uncovered for about 15 minutes.

Nutrition per serve	
Energy kJ (cals)	913 (218)
Protein	5 g
Total fat	8.3 g
Saturated fat	2.5 g
Fibre	5.7 g
Carbohydrate	31 mg
Cholesterol	<1 mg
Sodium	108 mg

Kiwi Fruit and Strawberry Salad with Ice Cream and Almond Toffee
High fibre, low GI

Combining golden kiwi fruit with green kiwi fruit and the strawberries really makes this into a gold star dessert. It is high in vitamin C, antioxidants, fibre and flavour. The almond toffee is easy and quick to prepare and really adds a delightful sweet crunch.

Preparation time: 10 minutes
Cooking time: 5 minutes
Serves: 2

1 tablespoon (15 g/½ oz) slivered almonds
3 teaspoons sugar
1 x 125 g/4½ oz green kiwi fruit, peeled and quartered
1 x 125 g/4½ oz golden kiwi fruit, peeled and quartered
250 g (9 oz) strawberries, hulled and halved
2 x 50 g/1¾ oz scoops low fat ice cream

Heat a small non-stick pan over a medium heat and cook the almonds, stirring, for 2–3 minutes or until golden. Spread in a single layer in a 10cm/4 inch circle on a baking tray covered with foil. Add the sugar to the pan and stir until dissolved and turns light golden brown, 1–2 minutes. Pour toffee over the almonds and leave to set. Place the kiwi fruit and strawberries in serving bowls with the ice-cream.

Break the toffee in half and place on the top of the ice cream.

Nutrition per serve	
Energy kJ (cals)	875 (209)
Protein	7.5 g
Total fat	6 g
Saturated fat	1.2 g
Fibre	7.5 g
Carbohydrate	31 g
Cholesterol	5 mg
Sodium	49 mg

Orange and Dried Fruit Salad with Orange Liqueur Yoghurt and an Orange, Mint and Liqueur Shot
High fibre, low GI

This dessert is particularly good to serve warm in winter but can be enjoyed at any time chilled. The fruit salad keeps well in the refrigerator and can be reheated in the microwave. The shot is deliciously refreshing to sip while enjoying the dessert and makes a very special finish to a dinner. If you prefer the dessert without the liqueur see the cook's note.

Preparation time: 5 minutes
Cooking time: 15 minutes
Storage time: 3 days refrigerated
Serves: 2

100 g/3½ oz dried fruit salad mix (prunes, apples, pears, peaches, apricots)

1 x 170 g/6 oz navel orange, peeled and cut into 8 wedges and trimmed

2 cinnamon quills, broken

1 cup (250 ml/9 fl oz) water

2 tablespoons (40 g/1½ oz) low fat vanilla yoghurt

1 teaspoon orange liqueur

½ cup (125 ml/4 fl oz) freshly squeezed orange juice

1 teaspoon orange liqueur, extra

½ teaspoon tiny mint leaves

2 sponge finger biscuits

Place the fruit salad, orange, cinnamon quills and water in a saucepan over a medium heat, cover and bring to the boil. Reduce the heat, and simmer for 10 minutes or until the fruit has plumped. Cool slightly.

Mix together the yoghurt and liqueur and chill until required. Pour the orange juice and extra liqueur into shot glasses and add the mint, chill until required.

Remove the cinnamon quills from the fruit salad and serve warm in bowls with a dollop of yoghurt and the shot and sponge finger on the side.

Cook's tip: Make this recipe alcohol-free by substituting the liqueur in the yoghurt with a little orange zest and a dash of honey to taste. Make the shot without the liqueur by adding orange zest with the mint to the juice.

Nutrition per serve	
Energy kJ (cals)	926 (221)
Protein	4.6 g
Total fat	0.9 g
Saturated fat	0.2 g
Fibre	6 g
Carbohydrate	47 g
Cholesterol	19 mg
Sodium	58 mg

Apples with Scrunched Filo and Maple Syrup Glazed Brazil Nuts
High fibre, low–medium GI

There are numerous recipes for apple pies as it is one of the most popular desserts especially when it is home made. This recipe looks stunning and it really does taste as good as it looks!

Preparation time: 15 minutes
Cooking time: 40 minutes
Serves: 2

2 x 200 g/7 oz cooking apples
2 teaspoons salt-reduced margarine spread
2 teaspoons 100% pure maple syrup
2 teaspoons lemon juice
¼ cup (60 ml/2 fl oz) water
2 teaspoons 100% pure maple syrup, extra
20g (¾ oz, 6 small) Brazil nuts
1 sheet commercial filo pastry chilled
A little icing sugar for sifting (¼–½ teaspoon)

Preheat oven to moderate180°C/350°F/Gas Mark 4 and line a baking tray with baking paper.

Peel, core and slice each apple into 12 wedges.

Heat the margarine spread in a non-stick frying pan over a low heat and arrange the apples in the pan in a single layer. Pour over the maple syrup and lemon juice. Cook the apples, moving them around during cooking to cook evenly and turning only once, for 35 minutes or until golden and tender. Add a little water during cooking if needed.

Place the water and extra maple syrup in a small non-stick pan over a medium heat and bring to the boil. Add the brazil nuts and continue to boil until the sauce has almost evaporated and the nuts are glazed, 2–3 minutes. Set aside.

Cut the sheet of filo pastry in half and scrunch each half up roughly. Place on the prepared baking tray and sift a little icing sugar on to each pastry. Bake for 1–2 minutes or until the filo is light golden.

Arrange the apple and Brazil nuts on serving plates with the filo on top.

Cook's note: Golden delicious or delicious apples are perfect for this recipe but any cooking apples can be used.

Nutrition per serve	
Energy kJ (cals)	997 (238)
Protein	2.7 g
Total fat	10.5 g
Saturated fat	2 g
Fibre	4.4 g
Carbohydrate	35 g
Cholesterol	0 mg
Sodium	67 mg

Anise Infused Rice Custard with Blood Orange
Medium GI

Preparation time: 10 minutes
Cooking time: 40 minutes
Chilling time: 30 minutes minimum
Serves: 2

1½ tablespoons (30 g/1 oz) medium grain brown rice
1 cup (250 ml/9 fl oz) water
1 teaspoon caster sugar
½ teaspoon ground cardamom
2 whole dried star anise
1 (50 g/1¾ oz) egg yolk
1½ teaspoons caster sugar, extra
1 teaspoon corn flour
½ cup (125 ml/4 fl oz) skim milk
A dash of vanilla extract to taste
1 (300 g/10½ oz) blood orange or orange, peeled and segmented

Place the rice, water, sugar, cardamom and star anise in a small saucepan over a medium heat. Bring to the boil, stirring occasionally. Reduce heat, cover and simmer for 20–25 minutes until the rice is almost tender. Increase the heat, uncover, and boil for a further 5–10 minutes or until the rice is tender and the liquid is absorbed, stirring constantly—take care not to allow all the water to evaporate before the rice is cooked—add a little more water if needed.

To make the custard, whisk the egg yolk in a small bowl with a fork and mix in the extra sugar. Set aside. Blend the corn flour with a little of the milk in a small saucepan. Stir in the remaining milk and heat over a medium/low heat, stirring constantly until hot—do not boil. Whisk the hot milk into the beaten egg and then pour the mixture back into the saucepan. Return to the heat and, stirring constantly to avoid any lumps, cook for about 1 minute or until the custard thickens and coats the back of a metal spoon—do not boil. Stir in the vanilla. Cover the surface of the custard with plastic wrap to prevent a skin forming and set aside.

Remove the star anise from the rice and add the custard, mixing well to incorporate all the flavours.

Spoon into two serving dishes and serve topped with the blood orange segments. In warm weather you might like to chill the custard before serving.

Cook's tip: A combination of citrus fruits segmented, such as lemon, lime and orange would be suitable to serve with the rice custard or try with nectarine, peach, apricot or mango when they are in season.

Nutrition per serve	
Energy kJ (cals)	723 (173)
Protein	6.4 g
Total fat	3 g
Saturated fat	0.9 g
Fibre	1.5 g
Carbohydrate	29 g
Cholesterol	91 mg
Sodium	41 mg

Baked Stone Fruits and Berries with Yoghurt and Honey
High fibre, low GI

This dessert can be popped into the oven while you are enjoying your main course and will be ready to serve when you are ready to enjoy it! The frozen berry mix we used in this dessert is high in antioxidants, containing bilberries, blackcurrants and wild blueberries.

Preparation time: 10 minutes
Cooking time: 20 minutes
Serves: 2

oil spray
2 x 125 g/4½ oz yellow peaches, stone
   removed and sliced
2 x 100 g/3½ oz yellow nectarines, stone
   removed and sliced
1 cup (150 g/5½ oz) frozen berry mix
1–2 teaspoons finely grated lemon zest
2 teaspoons brown sugar
¼ –½ teaspoon allspice
½ cup (125 g/4½ oz) low fat yoghurt
1 teaspoon honey

Preheat oven to moderate180°C/350°F/Gas Mark 4 and spray a flat ovenproof dish with oil. Arrange the peaches, nectarines and berries over the base of the dish. Sprinkle over the lemon zest, sugar and allspice. Cover the dish with foil and bake for 15 minutes.

Remove foil and stir and continue to cook for a further 5 minutes. Serve warm topped with yoghurt and drizzled with honey.

Nutrition per serve	
Energy kJ (cals)	690 (165)
Protein	7 g
Total fat	0.5 g
Saturated fat	<1g
Fibre	7.7 g
Carbohydrate	32 g
Cholesterol	3 mg
Sodium	50 mg

Further information

If you want to look into any topic in more detail, these will help you on your way.

Health

Heart health
Australia: www.heartfoundation.com.au
New Zealand: *www.nhf.org.nz*
USA: *www.americanheart.org*
UK: *www.bhf.org.uk*

General health
Australia: Commonwealth Department of Health (Australia) *www.health.gov.au*
New Zealand: Ministry of Health *http://www.moh.govt.nz/moh.nsf*
USA: *www.hhs.gov*

Diabetes
Australia: *www.diabetesaustralia.com.au*
New Zealand: *www.diabetes.org.nz*
USA: *www.diabetes.org*
UK: *www.diabetes.org.uk*

Find a dietitian
Australia: Dietitians Association of Australia *www.daa.asn.au*
New Zealand: New Zealand Dietetic Association *www.dietitians.org.nz*
USA: *www.eatright.org*
UK: *www.bda.uk.com*

Nutrition and food
Coffee and caffeine: *www.cosic.org*
Dairy foods: *www.dairyaustralia.com.au*
Egg Nutrition Advisory Group *http://www.enag.org.au*
Food Standards Australia and New Zealand *www.foodstandards.gov.au*
Fruit and vegetables: New Zealand campaign for the promotion of vegetables and fruit for health *http://www.5aday.co.nz/homepage.html*
Australian vegetables and fruit promotion *www.gofor2and5.com.au*
Beef and lamb information and cooking tips *www.themainmeal.com.au*
Information on nuts and health (including recipes) *www.nutsforhealth.com.au*
Plant sterol-enriched spreads: recipes and information
www.logicol.com.au/consumers/default.aspx
www.florapro-activ.com.au
Tea: *www.tea.co.uk*
Wholegrains: Go Grains *www.gograins.grdc.com.au*
Alcohol: Information site about alcohol from the Department of Health & Ageing *www.alcohol.gov.au*
Catherine Saxelby, Foodwatch: Expert nutrition advice and tips *www.foodwatch.com.au*
Nutrition Australia *www.nutritionaustralia.org*
Nutrition facts and analysis (U.S.A): *http://www.nutritiondata.com/index.html* Nutrition facts and analysis (U.S.A)
Portion sizes: This = that: a life-size photo guide to food serves, by Trudy Williams (2004). Publisher at Wesley Nutrition Centre, PO Box 383 Toowong Australia 4066 Ph +61 (7) 3870 8616 or visit *www.foodtalk.com.au*
Salt and health: *www.saltmatters.org*
USA food guide: *www.mypyramid.gov*

Dieting and weight loss

Dietitian, Australia: Dietitians Association of Australia
www.daa.asn.au

Dietitian, New Zealand: New Zealand Dietetic Association
www.dietitians.org.nz

Energy content of foods and online weight loss support:
www.calorieking.com.au

Expert tips and motivation on diet and exercise for weight loss
www.smartshape.com.au

Portion control and weight loss:

www.templatesystem.com.au

www.weightwatchers.com.au

Physical activity

Australian Association for Exercise and Sport Science
www.aaess.com.au

New Zealand physical activity guidelines
http://www.newhealth.govt.nz/toolkits/physical/guidelines.htm

Australian Council for Health, Physical Activity and Recreation
www.achper.org.au

Physical activity Guidelines for Australians
http://www.ausport.gov.au/fulltext/1999/feddep/physguide.pdf

Walking for health *www.10000steps.com.au*

Glycemic index

GI News (free e-newsletter): *http://ginews.blogspot.com*

Glycemic Index Database, plus information on GI and GL:
www.glycemicindex.com

Glycemic Index Symbol Program: *www.gisymbol.com.au*

Psychology

www.psychology.org.au

Sarah Edelman. *Change your thinking* (2002). ABC Books,
Australia

Eat to Beat Cholesterol is not just another diet or cook book. The authors are very well qualified and have incorporated the most recent evidence about fats and nutrients into this well set out book. Australia has new recommendations for the amount of nutrients we need to he prevent chronic diseases and this book includes these. It cuts through the clutter of information that can be found in the media. Nicole and Veronica present excellent tips for improving our diet, with easy and tempting recipes for meals that will fit into our busy lifestyles. Whether you have a cholesterol problem now or are interested in preventing heart disease there is something in this book for you.

Sandra Capra AM, PhD, FDAA
Professor of Nutrition and Dietetics
University of Newcastle.

Chronic degenerative diseases such as heart disease, stroke and type 2 diabetes have arisen as a result of changes in our environment. Diet and exercise are the most important changes that have affected our health. Nicole Senior and Veronica Cuskelly understand the importance of motivating readers to restore a healthy eating and exercise pattern by providing positive messages and understandable advice. Their recommendations concerning diet are well researched and up to date. They provide insights into the nutritional basis for food selection. They also include important information about the quantities of food which helps readers to avoid the tendency that we all have to over-eat. *Eat to Beat Cholesterol* provides a logical progression from scientific reasons to individual menus and practical recipes. It provides a very useful resource for health conscious members of the public and those who need to deal with cardiovascular risk factors.

Dr David Sullivan, physician and pathologist, Sydney

All over the world there are people who are living longer, happier and healthier lives than ever before. Everyone seems to agree that you should enjoy having a healthy life style and most of us are doing something about it.

Family history, we are told, has a lot to do with it. Today, it's not only a matter of inheritance; everyone can have a better life. Health, diet and fitness are part of today's way of thinking and we can take advantage of the many nutritionists and food writers who are dedicated to spreading the word about what we eat and why.

Nicole Senior a dietitian committed to good nutrition and Veronica Cuskelly an award winning food writer have put their clever heads together to share their beliefs, backed up by concrete knowledge that food is the best medicine, aware that when things go wrong there is an urgent cry for help.... straight from the heart. For that is what this book is all about, you and your heart.

They get to the heart of the matter explaining the cholesterol connection with timely advice on avoiding heartbreak.

The information is sound easy to understand and best of all it is interesting to read—for me a real page turner, not usual in a book of this nature.

Congratulations all round.

Margaret Fulton OAM

RECIPE INDEX

ABOUT THE AUTHORS

Nicole Senior is an Accredited Practising Dietitian (APD) and nutrition consultant with a passion for talking about the art and science of food in language everyone understands. As a nutrition expert, Nicole loves to cut through the clutter and provide do-able solutions that promote wellbeing and the joy of food.

Veronica Cuskelly is a freelance food consultant, home economist and an award-winning recipe writer. She has been developing and writing creative recipes for over twenty years and has written several cholesterol-lowering cookbooks. Veronica believes cooking and sharing great tasting food that is good for your heart increases the pleasure of eating.